PRAISE FOR *SHACKLED*

"*Shackled* unveils ICE's shadowy world, giving readers unique insight into both the inhumane removal process and the grueling work required to obtain even a modicum of justice for those in desperate need of protection. Rebecca Sharpless's meticulously detailed account of the harm they face is a must-read at a time when the basic rights of asylum seekers—especially those of color—are seriously eroding and calls to close our borders are louder than ever."

—CHERYL LITTLE, Cofounder and former Executive Director, Americans for Immigrant Justice

"I feel honored to have been invited into Abdulahi's and Sa'id's lives and to have learned about their struggles from an author who very evidently cares deeply about both of them. This book is heartbreaking. Using a lawyerly eye for detail and writing that is beautiful and deeply human, Sharpless delivers an incisive account of all that is wrong with the U.S. deportation system today."

—WILLIAM D. LOPEZ, author of *Separated: Family and Community in the Aftermath of an Immigration Raid*

"*Shackled* shows us a side of immigration crackdowns that even most immigration lawyers don't usually see: how deportation actually happens. It's an engaging, absurd, around-the-world journey of cruelty and resilience."

—MICHAEL KAGAN, author of *The Battle to Stay in America*

*Shackled*

*The publisher and the University of California Press Foundation gratefully acknowledge the generous support of the Anne G. Lipow Endowment Fund in Social Justice and Human Rights.*

# Shackled

## 92 REFUGEES IMPRISONED ON ICE AIR

Rebecca A. Sharpless

UNIVERSITY OF CALIFORNIA PRESS

University of California Press
Oakland, California

© 2024 by Rebecca Sharpless

Cataloging-in-Publication data is on file at the Library of Congress.

ISBN 978-0-520-39094-2 (cloth : alk. paper)
ISBN 978-0-520-39095-9 (pbk. : alk. paper)
ISBN 978-0-520-39865-8 (ebook)

Manufactured in the United States of America

33  32  31  30  29  28  27  26  25  24
10  9  8  7  6  5  4  3  2  1

Dedicated to the Group of 92
And to My Mother

# Contents

# *Preface*

This book is a story that had to be told. Writing it didn't feel like a choice. I was the custodian of the facts about personal backgrounds, the lawsuit, and immigration enforcement. If I didn't write it, no one would. After getting the go-ahead from Sa'id and Abdulahi, write it I did. At first in fits and starts. Then with determination.

The story is both shocking and unsurprising. In over decades of practicing immigration law, I had never been asked to help victims of such sustained and brutal mistreatment at the hands of ICE, U.S. Immigration and Customs Enforcement. At the same time, what happened must be understood as the preventable, natural consequence of the government's vast deportation machinery, including its routine practice of shackling people en masse and shipping them overseas in jumbo jet charter flights. This choice—one that no other country has made—makes the desperate and dangerous situation described in these pages almost inevitable.

This book tells the story of what happened to 92 people from Somalia on an ICE Air deportation flight, through the eyes of two men, Sa'id and Abdulahi. Many of the details come from my interviews with Sa'id and Abdulahi about their experiences on the ICE Air flight, and later in detention in the United States, as well as from interviews conducted by me of dozens of people on the flight, law students, and other advocates.

All events in this book are real, described by people who were present. Some facts come from documents, reports, my own observations, and official transcripts and recordings of court hearings. The timing of the events on the airport tarmac is approximate, having been reconstructed from the memories of Sa'id, Abdulahi, and other Somalis on the plane. Official transcripts and recordings document what was said in court. All other dialogue reflects what Sa'id, Abdulahi, and I, as well as others who were present, remember being said. I changed many of the names in the story to protect people's identity but there are no composite characters; each one is an actual person. The names of Abdulahi and Sa'id, and the names of their family members, are their own.

The group on the plane numbered 92—90 men and 2 women. I did not choose the stories of Sa'id and Abdulahi because they were more compelling than others. Each of the group of 92 has a story worth telling and that someday I hope will be told. People may wonder why I didn't write in detail about the two women on the plane. One woman, a mother of a young child, was released after the legal team discovered that she should not have been ordered deported in the first place. The second woman's story was so heartbreaking that I could not bring myself to ask her to share it with the world.

Finally, I must express my profound regret for not taking Abdulahi's case when he had his chance to reopen it. I was aware of his situation and the delay in getting the needed legal paperwork filed. Yet I did not step in to handle his case myself—a mistake I must live with.

# PART I

# 1 *ICE Air*

Alexandria, Louisiana

DECEMBER 6, 2017

*ICE Air Operations: The "air transportation" department of U.S. Immigration and Customs Enforcement (ICE) that "facilitate[s] the movement of noncitizens within the United States and the removal of noncitizens to destinations worldwide."*

WEBSITE OF IMMIGRATION AND CUSTOMS ENFORCEMENT

Sa'id Abdi Janale waited in line for one of the three working telephones in the Louisiana immigration jail's dayroom. Banks of fluorescent lights cast cold light from the low ceiling onto rectangular metal tables down the middle of the room, each flanked by stools bolted to the floor. A TV hung over the tables, out of reach. Sa'id—tall with cropped hair and brown eyes—wore tan leather loafers, khaki pants, and a white polo shirt. These were the same clothes he had worn when immigration officers arrested him four months earlier. Sa'id surveyed the scene, hands at his side. His calm contrasted with the edginess of others in the room. In front of him, other men bound for Somalia bowed their heads and spoke into the phones in hushed but frantic tones. The calls were time-limited, expensive, and recorded, but they were lifelines connecting these men to families they might never see again. A white plane with red markings spelling

Omni Air International was visible through the room's window, a Boeing 767 jumbo jet. In the still darkness of the evening, a spotlight shined down on the nose of the plane, casting a shadow on the tarmac. Sa'id feared he would be on that plane in the morning.

Sa'id was one of 90 men and 2 women born in Somalia who were jailed together at the private prison known as the Alexandria Staging Facility, located in central Louisiana, a three-and-a-half hour drive from New Orleans. Immigration officials had shipped them here from jails around the country to deport them as a group. Charter flight N225AX would carry them away early the next day. Each of the 92 had a final order of removal. The United States would ship them back to their country of birth in chains, although lawyers would later find that many had sound defenses to deportation that no court had ever considered.

Sa'id reached the front of the phone line. He gripped the telephone receiver and winced as his pinky finger connected with the still-warm, black plastic. An injury from another immigration jail made its presence known. Sa'id pressed the familiar numbers, wondering what prefix he would have to add to the 617 Massachusetts area code when dialing from Somalia. The United States was forcing him to return a country that was his in name only. After his father was shot in front of him during Somalia's civil war, Sa'id had fled at age five with his mother, brothers, and sisters. He had no one left in Somalia. The war that began in 1991 had left his entire family either dead or scattered across Kenyan refugee camps.

Sa'id's mother had remarried during her six years in the camps. Her second husband, an artist, had painted a mural of a well-known shipwreck on a wall at one of the three camps where they took shelter. Overcome by turbulent water off the coast of Kenya, the passengers, Somalis fleeing the civil war, stretched out their arms for help that would not arrive. Of the 700 on the overloaded boat, more than 150 perished. Most did not know how to swim. The sudden calamity at sea contrasted with the slowly unfolding human tragedy within the camp amid the mud and tents. Sa'id kept a small replica of the painting as a reminder of the long years he spent hungry and hot as a young child, moving from camp to camp, as well as the importance of the sea to his fishermen family. The picture hung in the bedroom of the Boston-area home he shared with his wife, Janene Johnson, a U.S. citizen.

Sa'id had always loved art—he carried favorite images with him. As a teenager in Dallas, he defied his mother and stepfather to imprint his body with the name of his mother, Maryan. Now tattoos, including the names and portraits of his children, covered much of his arms and chest. His right arm bore the word "solo" outlined by a map of the place he called home, Texas. On his chest, he had inked "Only Allah can judge me." A clock and an hourglass signified the fleeting nature of time.

In the United States, Sa'id's body art expressed his connection to his family, his religion, his home of two decades, and his feeling of being alone, caught between Somali and American culture. In Somalia, it would mark him a target of al-Shabaab—an al-Qaeda–aligned group on a mission to establish a state in Somalia based on a distorted version of Islam. Emerging from the ashes of Somalia's brutal civil war, al-Shabaab had displaced Somalia's weak central government in large swaths of the country. Just two months before Sa'id took his place in the Alexandria jail phone line, the group had killed over 500 people in Mogadishu in a bombing attack known as the "Somali 9/11."

As a Somali associated with the United States, Sa'id faced profound danger in his birth country. Al-Shabaab forbids tattoos and would punish the "Allah" tattoo as an extreme affront. It would be impossible to hide Sa'id's outsider status, not only because of the tattoos but because he, like many who came to the United States as children, spoke Somali with a pronounced American accent and had no current knowledge of Somalia. Sa'id was what some Somalis refer to as "say walahi"—a phrase that means "I swear to God" or, when posed as a question, "Swear to God?" Americanized Somalis are "say walahi," because they tend to use this phrase more than other Somalis.

Sa'id leaned his left forearm on the jail phone kiosk to steady himself. Janene answered on the first ring.

"Anything from the immigration lawyer?" Sa'id almost whispered the question.

"Nothing," said Janene. "He didn't answer the phone. I went to his office, and he didn't open the door. We paid $7,000 for nothing." Up until that moment, Sa'id had believed something could be done—some legal maneuver—to stop his deportation. But now he was coming to understand that the fee they had paid the lawyer could have gone to take care of the children or to help him survive in Somalia.

Sa'id and Janene tried to match the conversation to the moment. She insisted she would move the family to be with him, that they would find a way. Sa'id smiled at her optimism as he looked at the cement floor. He knew better. Janene and the children could not live in Somalia, a war-torn country with a barely functioning government. Even visiting would be all but impossible. The U.S. Federal Aviation Administration had barred U.S. airlines from flying to Somalia for fear of a terrorist attack at the airport.

All Sa'id could cling to, during this last night before deportation, was a semblance of normalcy. He yearned for the day-to-day, to be at home with his family. "How are the boys?" he asked.

"OK. Robbie keeps asking when you will be back. It hasn't sunk in yet. I'm dreading what it will be like when it does." Janene had been a single mother of two when Sa'id met her. Robbie was now in first grade. Cerebral palsy kept Janene's eight-year-old, Jailen, out of regular school. Janene could no longer lift her growing son. It had been Sa'id who bathed and fed Jailen and cleared mucus from his mouth when he had trouble breathing at night.

"How is the baby?" From his pocket, Sa'id took out the photo of Sa'id Jr. that Janene had mailed to him. He had missed his son's birth because he was in immigration custody. He ran his thumb over the picture of his three-month-old son. At Sa'id's request, Janene had printed photos at Walgreens. It was all they could do to try and bridge the gap between separated father and son.

"He had a good night, thank goodness. But breastfeeding is still hard. He's not latching on well. My breasts are so full of milk they hurt."

The sounds of raised voices speaking in Somali caught Sa'id's attention. He turned from the phone to see what was happening in the middle of the room. Men converged into a large group, gesturing with their hands. Before Sa'id could make out what they were saying, an officer approached, pointing to the telephones and shaking his head. "No more phone calls," he snapped in English. "Get to your cell."

Sa'id didn't want to hang up. He had no way of knowing when he would next talk with Janene. But he had no choice. Officers were shutting down the dayroom for the night.

Sa'id slid the phone back on the hook and took a few slow steps toward the gathering crowd. Dozens of the men, all slated for the next morning's flight, were speaking in a mix of Somali and English, their voices pitched to the urgency of their impending deportation. Some were seated on the stools and tables, but most stood, facing a correctional officer. Sa'id stood with them.

Each morning, over 20,000 men, women, and children wake up in 200 immigration detention centers across the United States. The Alexandria Staging Facility is one of about 150 U.S. immigration jails run by private prison corporations. Built in 2013 at the behest of the federal government, the Louisiana facility contracts with Immigration and Customs Enforcement to incarcerate people before they board ICE Air flights—charter deportation flights paid for by the government. The "new state of the art transfer center provides efficiency of [sic] the ICE removal process," explains the Alexandria Staging Facility's website.

The jail resembles a large warehouse. A rectangular metal roof spans the one-story concrete-block structure, which has a capacity of 400 "beds," or "bodies" in law-enforcement parlance. People spend the day in a common area, where they eat and watch TV. They sleep in locked, two-person cells flanking this dayroom. Each cell measures 8' × 10' and has a metal bunk bed and an open steel toilet in the corner. Deportation planes use a full-size airstrip alongside the jail. ICE officers walk people out of the facility, across the tarmac, and up the aircraft stairs.

GEO Group, the second largest private prison company in the United States, owns and operates Alexandria Staging Facility. The federal government, including ICE, is GEO Group's largest client. Fueled by the country's zero-tolerance immigration enforcement policy, business was booming. The company incarcerates tens of thousands of people for ICE at a price tag of over $600 million a year. The day after Donald Trump was elected in 2016, GEO Group's stock rose 21 percent, soaring to 98 percent by three months after the election.

Before Sa'id could hear what the men were saying, he could read what was happening. None of them wanted to be sent into the cells for the night. Even if they managed to fall asleep, they would have to get up in a few hours for the predawn deportation flight. The men wanted this time to talk and absorb the enormity of what was about to happen to them. To plan. To try and cope. After his conversation with Janene had been cut short, Sa'id felt the same way. But his many months in detention had taught him the correctional playbook. A group of detained men making a request, even a reasonable one, would be seen by the jail authorities as a threat to officer safety and shut down, usually with an order to disperse into the cells. Any resistance, even verbal, could trigger violence. As a large Black man, Sa'id had to be careful.

Nonetheless, he risked an intervention. He thought of himself as an American, and he knew he spoke like one. "Officer, we only have a few hours before the flight. Can we stay up?"

"We still have not seen the travel documents from the Somali Embassy," added Omar, another man slated to be on the flight.

Omar was older than most of the other men. He had a gray beard and walked with a cane. He spoke fluent English. A few days before, a woman from the Somali Embassy in Washington, DC, had assured Omar and others that no travel documents had been issued. Now, Omar pressed his point with the correctional officer at the Alexandria jail. "It's not legal," he said, "for ICE to deport us without travel documents." Omar and the other men hoped that the embassy was telling the truth and would stand up for them by refusing to issue travel documents until the dangerous conditions in Somalia improved. But knowing that the embassy was corrupt, weak, and unskilled at diplomacy with the United States, the men did not have high expectations.

Sa'id watched the correctional officer's face as he considered the request to let them stay up and what it might take to force the dozens of men into the cells.

The officer called the jail warden.

Joseph Jackson was at home when the report came that a group of African men were refusing to return to the cells. A former Marine, Jackson's correctional career had spanned more than 30 years. It was not the first time he had been called to manage a brewing disturbance at a jail. He put on his warden uniform and drove to the jail. As he entered the dayroom, he saw the men standing and talking—their discussion heated but, he knew, not a threat. He walked toward them, by himself, his hands empty.

The men fell silent.

"Good evening," Jackson said. "I understand that you don't want to go to bed." He stood before the men, eying them steadily. He listened as Sa'id and others explained. After a nod and a pause, he addressed the group with a practiced calm. "Gentlemen, I am asking you not to create a problem in my jail. Please respect each other and my jail. I am not ICE. I have no control over your deportation. In the morning, ICE will show you your travel documents before you get on the plane. You can stay up."

One of the men asked, "Can we have coffee?"

Jackson nodded yes.

The men thought that the warden, as a Black man himself, could feel their pain. Jackson could have summoned the jail's SWAT team, but he didn't. Sa'id and the others felt they had secured a small victory.

In another wing of the Alexandria Staging Facility, Abdulahi Hassan Mohumed lay motionless on the top bunk of the cell he shared with Ali, another Somali man. Like Sa'id, Abdulahi and Ali were slated to be deported on the next day's deportation flight. Unlike Sa'id, Abdulahi and Ali preferred to rest before the long journey. Abdulahi turned on his side to face the blank wall of the cell and pulled the jail-issued sheet and thin blanket up and over his body. He closed his eyes and tried to shut out thoughts of Somalia and fall asleep.

Two years before, Abdulahi had arrived at the U.S.-Mexico border to ask for asylum. He was 28, skinny, and soft-spoken. Through his sincere tone and few words of English, he managed to communicate his plea: In Somalia, his parents had been killed, his sister raped, and he had been kidnapped. Although he had escaped to South Africa, where he had lived for ten years, he was still not safe. His first wife had been killed, and he had been injured, in a xenophobic mob attack. He had no visa to enter the United States, but could he please apply for asylum? Abdulahi was invoking his right under international law to seek protection as a refugee.

U.S. protection law is rooted in the international human rights principle of non-refoulement or non-return. From the French verb refouler, "to force back," the principle forbids governments from returning people to countries where their life or freedom would likely be threatened. This bedrock, mandatory duty of nations has roots in the eighteenth-century philosophy of Immanuel Kant, who argued that people have a moral duty to help others, even if they are strangers, provided doing so does not endanger the giver of aid. Kant's principle of hospitality entitles strangers seeking entry into a community the right to enter temporarily without being treated as enemies, if turning the strangers away would lead to their deaths. The prohibition on refoulement appeared for the first time in a major international law document in the 1933 League of Nations Convention Relating to the International Status of Refugees. If the United States had recognized the principle in 1939, it might not have blocked the M.S. *St. Louis*—a ship filled with Jewish families fleeing Nazi Germany—from docking in Miami.

The genocide of World War II moved the international community to establish the United Nations and commit to guaranteeing all people certain human rights. In 1948, the United Nations adopted the Universal Declaration of Human Rights. Three years later, the United Nations Convention Relating to the Status of Refugees codified principles to govern the treatment of refugees, including the principle of non-refoulement. Under Article 33 of the Convention, "No Contracting State shall expel or return (refouler) a refugee in any manner whatsoever to the frontiers of territories where his life or freedom would be threatened on account of his race, religion, nationality, membership of a particular social group or political opinion." President Truman declined to sign the Convention, believing it infringed on U.S. sovereignty. Twenty years later, President Johnson, citing "the American heritage of concern for the homeless and persecuted," persuaded Congress to give its advice and consent to the 1967 Protocol Relating to the Status of Refugees, which incorporated Article 33 of the Convention. The protection enshrined in Article 33 now appears in domestic immigration law in the Immigration and Nationality Act.

So Abdulahi had a right to apply for protection, but the United States, unlike other countries, chooses to lock up many asylum seekers while they pursue their cases. He would have to petition for asylum from a jail cell, and it would take a long time. Abdulahi's asylum case dragged on for weeks, then months, and then a full two years before it made its way from the immigration judge in Georgia to an administrative appeals court, which made the final decision—a denial. It was not unusual for an immigration case, or an immigrant's incarceration, to stretch so long. Nor was the denial in Abdulahi's case surprising. Despite the gut-wrenching violence in Somalia, Somali asylum cases are hard to win. It's not enough that a person reasonably fear being harmed. The feared violence must be on account of one of the five grounds for asylum—political opinion, race, religion, nationality, or membership in a particular social group. And the rules are daunting for when a person's testimony must be supported by other, more objective, evidence. Most importantly, the odds of winning have as much to do with the law as they do with the judge who hears the case. The disparities in adjudications are so extreme that advocates refer to the asylum system as "refugee roulette."

Unlike Sa'id, Abdulahi was an asylum seeker and had never been at liberty in the United States. For two years, correctional officers had controlled every aspect of Abdulahi's existence, from the 5:30 a.m. wake-up to TV-off at 11 p.m. His chance to eat and take one hour of fresh air per day all occurred on a schedule. Jail administrators rationed everything from small bottles of liquid soap and toilet paper to food and medical care. Abdulahi could not even find silence. The clanking of metal doors, alarms, and buzzers, and the din of the television and other detained men's voices, often raised and sometimes shouting, meant it was never quiet inside the detention center's concrete walls.

During his two years in detention, Abdulahi did his best to keep busy, always the first to volunteer to work in the kitchen or the laundry room or to clean the bathrooms. He worked hard, just like he had running small stores during his time in South Africa, but for only pennies of compensation. He needed the meager earnings to fund his jail commissary account to pay for phone calls, extra soap and shampoo, and the occasional snack. He also worked because he understood the value of distraction to surviving detention.

On the morning of his scheduled deportation from the Alexandria Staging Facility, Abdulahi was asleep when a correctional officer banged open his cell door at 2:30 a.m. The officer entered, gripping a tangle of wrist and leg chains to shackle Abdulahi and Ali for the flight. Abdulahi sat up and eased himself down from the upper bunk. He was no stranger to being in irons. All he—and so many other asylum seekers detained by ICE—had done was ask the United States to protect him. Nonetheless, ICE agents fastened metal cuffs and chains around Abdulahi's wrists, waist, and legs every time they transported him anywhere, even to see a doctor. Abdulahi had become skilled at playing the pleasant prisoner, hoping the correctional officers would not ratchet the shackles too tight, hurl racial slurs, or shove him around. But the constant performance was exhausting, and he remained at their mercy.

For thousands of years, humans have asserted power and authority over others through cuff-like restraints. Greek myths refer to "fetters," as do the Bible and the Qur'an. ICE has a list of handcuffs approved for use on people in its custody. The September 2017 list of Authorized Restraint Devices included Hiatt-Thompson 2010 Chain Link Cuffs. Founded in 1780, the British company Hiatt first mass-produced restraints for the American slave industry. Its handcuffs from the mid-1800s incorporated a short chain that tethered two U-shaped cuffs with a locking hinged bar across the end to encircle the wrists of enslaved people. A hunting and outdoor website selling the handcuffs describes the company's legacy: "Similar to when the restraints were built hundreds of years ago in England, today's Hiatt handcuffs are designed to meet the needs of law enforcement personnel through a variety of unique features."

The evolution of modern handcuffs has focused on law-enforcement convenience rather than the safety or comfort of the people who wear them. In the early twentieth century, law enforcement started using swing cuffs, the predecessor to today's handcuffs. Swing shackles are hinged metal bands that close on teeth inside. The spring system in the swing design allows quick one-handed shackling. A squeeze activates the one-way ratchet, making the cuffs easy to tighten. Loosening requires unlocking with a key. Some modern cuffs use a central metal piece to make them rigid once locked in place, restricting independent hand movement. Instead of a rigid connector, some cuffs use a short chain that joins the wrist shackles and a second chain that tethers the cuffs to the restrained person's waist, allowing limited range of motion.

Prior to 2012, ICE shackled people during transportation only after an individual assessment that considered a person's age, sex, physical or medical conditions, criminal history, behavior patterns, and potential influence of drugs or alcohol. Regulations required officers to give an "articulated reason" for using shackles. Then, during the Obama Administration, ICE adopted an across-the-board policy of shackling. This shift coincided with a growing reliance on charter flights—a way to efficiently deport large numbers of people while keeping the process in the shadows—and a dramatic increase in deportations. Deportations had multiplied by a factor of 13, from 30,000 in the late 1990s to 400,000 in 2016. ICE Air Operations— the government unit in charge of deportations by plane—switched from buying tickets on commercial flights to contracting with private charter companies. In 2016, ICE spent $95 million on charters, compared to $21 million on commercial flights in the same year.

ICE's across-the-board shackling policy is at odds with medical evidence on the physical effects of restraints. Swing handcuffs easily compress the superficial radial nerve in the wrist, potentially damaging the nerves and leading to numbness or weakness. A study by the Emory University School of Medicine published in 2000 found that these effects can last for weeks or months and may even be permanent. The maximum time people in the study were shackled was six hours, with most being restrained for about an hour and a half. A 2015 medical study recommended, "Handcuffs should be applied for as short a time as possible and be tightened only to the extent that they achieve the restraint or control needed." Abdulahi, Sa'id, and the other 90 Somali men and women leaving Alexandria Staging Facility would be cuffed for almost two days.

The officer motioned for Abdulahi and Ali to sit on the bottom bunk and put on their own ankle cuffs. He ordered them to stand, fastened chains around their waist and cuffed their hands. Then the officer connected the chain-linked handcuffs to their waist chains and left. Because ICE would be shackling Abdulahi and Ali for many hours, the officer allowed them a few inches of arm reach so that he could eat and use the bathroom without assistance. But the restraints prevented Abdulahi from climbing back onto the upper bunk, so he sat on the lower bunk next to Ali. Their heads bobbed with fatigue; their chains clanked whenever they moved.

There was nothing to do but wait.

At 4:30 a.m., another officer entered the cell, clicking the men's wrist and ankle chains tighter before he ordered them out. It was time to go. Abdulahi flinched, stood up, and started walking, struggling to approximate a natural gait down the hall and through the door that led onto the tarmac. His mind drifted to a question he had asked himself often during his two years in immigration detention: Am I a person anymore? As the officer herded him and the others toward the plane, Abdulahi felt less and less like a man and more like cargo.

The early morning air was cool but sticky. Nothing was visible beyond the tarmac in the predawn darkness, no trees or vegetation. A breeze carried the smell of jet fuel and the sounds of officers shouting orders. The noise of leg chains in motion accompanied Abdulahi and his fellow prisoners as they walked single-file toward the plane. Illuminated by the red lights of law enforcement SUVs, the jet loomed large. It dwarfed the file of men and women shuffling toward it—an ordinary airplane transformed into a flying cage.

Operated by the private charter company Omni Air International, the Boeing 767 jet could seat 215 along two aisles, typical for an international flight. The Oklahoma-based company was angling for more work from the federal government, having already profited in the millions from lucrative military defense contracts. Deportation contracts flow to Omni Air through flight brokers, including CSI Aviation and Classic Air Charter, which contract with ICE Air. According to Classic Air Charter, Omni Air is the "sole-source carrier" for "special high-risk charter" flights, which was code for deportation flights for Black African men. For a single deportation flight in 2019, Omni Air would charge ICE a whopping $33,500 per hour. According to Classic Air Charter, Omni had been able to "monopolize the market" because other carriers, were "discouraged by the potential of public backlash or negative media attention."

The jail warden, Joseph Jackson, had spared the Somali men from the jail's SWAT team the night before. Now, ICE's own SWAT unit, the Special Response Team or SRT, was deployed in full force. Dozens of SRT officers in full riot gear lined the tarmac. Officers in body armor and helmets with face shields, holding sticks and body-length shields yelled orders, "Keep moving. Stay in line." The officers tied black bags over the heads of ten of the shackled men. Made of black mesh with solid fabric covering the men's noses and mouths, these "transport hoods" were designed for prisoners who have a history of spitting at officers, although nothing in the background of the men suggested this extraordinary type of restraint was needed. As Abdulahi neared the plane, he saw a straitjacket, called the WRAP, spread out on the ground. ICE had arranged for an overwhelming show of force to send a message to the Black men they presumed were dangerous: "Don't resist. Don't ask questions. Do as you are told, or you will be hurt." His memory flashed to when he was 18 years old in Somalia and kidnappers were pulling a burlap sack over his head. Abdulahi began to sweat.

When he reached the bottom of the aircraft stairs, two officers placed their hands on his shoulders and pushed him hard up the metal steps. "Move it!" one barked. Abdulahi was already obeying the officers. He wondered why they were so scared of him. The only threat he had ever posed to anyone was on the soccer field.

Abdulahi ducked to enter the plane door and shuffled down the aisle, trying not to trip on his shackles. He looked toward the back of the plane, to the faces of men and women, bound and herded together. Several met his gaze, then looked away. These were his people, together about to lose part of their humanity as the most powerful nation shipped them to the other side of the world.

Abdulahi kept moving. After a few rows, an ICE officer directed him into an aisle seat.

Two dozen rows behind Abdulahi, Sa'id leaned forward. He stared out the window, past the reflection of his face illuminated by the cabin lights and into the blackness. There was no trace of dawn. The plane began to move, picking up speed until it lifted into the air.

Twenty years earlier, in 1997, 11-year-old Sa'id had landed at the Dallas Fort Worth International Airport, with his mother and siblings.

Unlike Abdulahi, Sa'id and his family had entered the United States with legal immigration status as refugees, based on the violence they had endured in war-torn Somalia. Life in the United States was a big adjustment for Sa'id. The pace, culture, and expectations were all so different from the refugee camps where he grew up. In Texas, he had endured bullying and corporal punishment at school and struggled to succeed in the classroom. Even after he learned to speak English, reading was a special challenge. But he stuck with his education until 2004, when, at age 18, the demands of family overtook him. His girlfriend, Tiffany, was pregnant with their first child, Layla. Sa'id dropped out of school to save up money to pay for an apartment for the three of them, landing a job with a car rental company at the Dallas airport. As the main breadwinner of his new family, he often worked overtime on the weekends to try and make ends meet. In the next years, Sa'id and Tiffany had two more children, Nyla and Mohamed.

To the Somali community in Dallas, Sa'id had been an outsider. Tiffany was not Muslim, and Sa'id drank alcohol, something prohibited by Islam. Sa'id felt judged not only for living with Tiffany and drinking but for his American style of dress and his choice of American friends, considered a bad influence. As a young teen, Sa'id and his brother Mohammed went every Friday to play indoor soccer with other Somali boys. But everyone treated Sa'id as if he had been born in the United States. Eventually, Mohammed asked Sa'id to stop going to play soccer.

First as a child and then as an adult, Sa'id got in trouble with the law. He spent time in jail, away from Tiffany and the kids. The end of Sa'id's relationship with Tiffany came on New Year's Eve 2011, after the police stopped him for driving while intoxicated. He was sentenced to 100 days in jail, and Tiffany left him.

Sa'id tried to make a fresh start. When his uncle Abdulahi Ahmed, nicknamed "Never" in the refugee camps, offered him a construction job in Boston, he took the opportunity, reluctant as he was to leave Texas. Dallas was home, and Sa'id was worried about not seeing his children. But he couldn't turn down the promise of steady and well-paid work. In September of 2011, Sa'id flew to Boston. He had lived in Texas almost twice as long as he had in Africa.

In Boston, Sa'id lived and worked with his uncle. The construction job was demanding. He got up every morning at 4:30 to climb up unstable ladders to work on roofs. Sa'id started a new relationship with Khadija, a nurse, and they had a daughter named Maryan, named for Sa'id's mother. They lived in a two-bedroom apartment in Somerville. Sa'id kept up his relationship with his kids in Texas, flying them out to spend summers with him and Khadija. He enjoyed taking his children to the local pool, the Boston aquarium, and Six Flags amusement park, although he was too scared to ride the roller coasters.

In 2013, Sa'id's relationship with Khadija began to falter, and, while they were separated, Sa'id was convicted of trying to break into their car. The car was in Khadija's name, but Sa'id was making the payments. Sa'id got into more trouble when, during Boston's long winter storms, he worked for a man who had a small crew that shoveled snow for businesses. The contractor paid him in large bills that turned out to be fake. Sa'id was arrested for trying to use the bills and was put on probation.

Things turned around in 2015. Sa'id met Janene—warm, outgoing, and successful. At first, he wondered what she saw in him. They brought out the best in each other, and soon Sa'id and Janene were living together with her two young sons, Robbie and Jailen. Sa'id worked long hours in construction. His skills expanded beyond roof repair to bathroom tiling and carpet installation. All was well until Sa'id reported late to his probation officer, prompting a judge to order him jailed for the weekend. At the time, ICE was monitoring people in jail, matching their fingerprints against immigration databases. Despite Sa'id having lawful immigration status, ICE could seek to deport him based on his Massachusetts convictions for breaking into the car he shared with Khadija and the counterfeit bills. With that, Sa'id's immigration troubles began, 19 years after he arrived in the United States as a refugee.

ICE booked Sa'id into the Suffolk County jail in Boston, a local jail with a federal contract to hold people slated for deportation. Sa'id appeared by himself before the immigration judge, Steven Day. He could not afford a lawyer, and the court's list of free legal services was a dead end. Although Sa'id was eligible to file an application, called a refugee waiver, to stop his deportation based on hardship to his family, no one, not even Judge Day, told him this. Instead, an ICE officer assured Sa'id he would be released immediately if he accepted the deportation order without fighting his case. The United States was not deporting people to Somalia, the officer explained, because conditions there were too dangerous. The Somali Embassy would confirm that it was not issuing the required travel documents. For deportations to Somalia to proceed, the U.S. immigration authorities needed the Somali Embassy to issue a passport or other official travel document proving Sa'id was Somali. With the political situation worsening in Somalia, it appeared deportations would be halted for a long time. If he took the deportation officer's advice, Sa'id would end up with a final deportation order against him, but ICE would allow him to remain and work in the United States until conditions improved in Somalia, which seemed unlikely, if not impossible. Meanwhile, Sa'id could get out of jail and return to his family.

Despite these assurances, Sa'id had misgivings, as did Janene. Over the jail phone, they discussed the terrible choice he had to make—give up his case in court to be released or stay in jail while fighting the case. There was no easy answer. It seemed unwise to give up his case in court, but ICE insisted that accepting the deportation order was the quickest way out. Judge Day had already denied Sa'id a bond, in a five-minute hearing, because of his criminal record. Sa'id could hear the desperation in Janene's voice when they spoke—she and the boys needed him. He decided to accept the order of deportation, and ICE released him a few months later. He left the jail and returned to his life with Janene. Sa'id picked up with his former life, working and being a father. Soon, Janene announced she was pregnant with their first child. Maybe the nightmare really was over.

In 2017, just months after Sa'id's release from immigration jail, ICE resumed deportations to Somalia, even though Somalia was no safer than before. Immigration officers took Sa'id back into custody in August. Janene gave birth to Sa'id Jr. two weeks later. He felt cheated. Giving up his court case for less than a year of liberty seemed a poor bargain. He was now on the brink of being shipped across the Atlantic to a country he had not seen since he was five years old, running from his father's murderers. Janene would be left raising her boys and their baby without him.

Sa'id, now 31, drew a long breath and exhaled slowly as the engines of the airplane roared to life at 5:45 a.m. He agonized over whether he would ever see Janene and the kids again. It was hard to fathom that the United States considered his criminal record serious enough to rip him away from his wife and children, from the life he had built.

As the plane broke through the clouds, the yellow sodium lights of the Alexandria jail disappeared from view. Despite the promise of the Alexandria jail's warden, ICE had not shown any of the men and women on board the plane the promised Somali travel documents.

Sa'id had never heard of anyone being brought back to the United States after a deportation flight took off. It just didn't happen. He stared into the dark sky. He was on an airship filled with Black men and women chained and bound for Africa—a reverse Middle Passage.

It would take a miracle to save them now.

## 2   *On the Tarmac*

Dakar, Senegal

DECEMBER 7, 2017

*Dakar, the capital city of Senegal, on the west coast of Africa, is over 4,000 miles from Mogadishu, the capital city of Somalia, located on Africa's east coast.*

Nine hours after taking off from Louisiana, ICE Air Flight N225AX touched down on schedule at 7:30 p.m. Senegal time, at the Blaise Diagne International Airport on the outskirts of Dakar. The first leg of the journey was complete. The group of 92 had already been shackled for 12 hours, nine hours of flight time plus three in jail prior to the flight.

Sa'id peered through the plane window. The lights in the air traffic control tower gleamed in the evening darkness. The modern curves of the terminal building looked brand new. In fact, it was the day of the airport's grand opening. Flight N225AX was one of the first to land on the new runway. During the opening ceremony hours earlier, Senegal's president, Macky Sall, and other leaders, had gathered to watch dancers draped in dazzling yellow and orange costumes perform on the airport grounds. The $600-million airport had been 10 years in the making. The ceremony had drawn a large crowd, but now the tarmac was quiet.

Seated toward the rear of the plane, Sa'id yawned and tried to stretch out his shackled legs in front of him. Next to him sat Nadim, a man in his 20s who Sa'id had befriended a week earlier in immigration detention. Like Sa'id, Nadim had grown up in the United States after he and his siblings had entered as refugees. With no parents in the United States, Nadim had become homeless as a teenager and was in and out of jail.

An hour passed. Still, the plane did not move. Another hour passed.

An officer finally announced over the intercom, "Our departure is delayed. We need to wait for a part from the United States to fix the plane."

Sa'id didn't know what to think. He turned to Nadim and sighed. "A part from the U.S.? Really?"

"Right," said Nadim, shaking his head. "I don't know how much more of this I can take." He spoke for them both.

Sa'id shifted, trying to settle into the waiting. His frame took up every inch of the seat. Though its passengers were bound hand and foot, the chartered flight offered seatback in-flight entertainment. Sa'id tried without success to focus on an X-men movie. He found some music, trying to lose himself in an Ariana Grande song as he imagined what Janene would say: "Stay positive. Think about the kids." Sa'id wished he had met Janene earlier in his life. Her influence might have kept him out of jail. But he blamed only himself for his current predicament.

He could find no way to ease the increasing pain of the shackles that dug into his wrists, waist, and ankles. His ankles had swollen during the flight, leaving no space between his skin and the metal. ICE officers at the Alexandria Staging Facility had promised him there were larger shackles on the plane, which could be swapped in after they took off. Another lie.

Sa'id tried not to focus on the physical pain and, instead, to come to grips with what lay ahead. He had $80 in his pocket and no connections. U.S. officials were about to drop him into a country the United States itself considered one of the most dangerous places in the world. The Department of State was warning travelers against visiting Somalia, citing crime, civil unrest, kidnapping, and piracy. ICE did not dare send its own officers to Somalia. After the layover in Dakar, Flight N225AX was scheduled to fly the Somali men and women 4,000 miles east, across the African continent to Djibouti, where they would be passed off to Jubba Airways, a Somali airline, for the final, shorter leg south to Mogadishu.

Far from Sa'id, Abdulahi was seated at the front of the plane, across the aisle from his friend Ibrahim. With his seat reclined, Abdulahi had closed his eyes and was trying to relax. When the announcement came that they would have to wait for a part from the United States to fix the plane, Abdulahi opened his eyes and sat up straight. He and Ibrahim exchanged glances. "Don't stress. It will be okay," said Ibrahim.

Abdulahi watched the flight nurses take advantage of the layover in Senegal to dispense medication. Some of the group of 92 Somali men and women suffered from diabetes and required injections. Others needed psychotropic medication for mental health conditions. Under government regulations, the medical staff was also supposed to monitor the effect of the shackles and tend to any medical issues or injuries during the flight—duties they would later neglect.

Although Abdulahi had met Ibrahim only a few days earlier, when ICE moved them to the Alexandria Staging Facility, Ibrahim had become a calming influence on him. Ibrahim was older and spoke fluent English. He could explain things about the United States that Abdulahi did not understand. Unlike Abdulahi, whose entire time in the country had been in immigration detention, Ibrahim had lived in the United States for decades. He, his wife, and their three children made their home in Atlanta, where Ibrahim worked as a mechanic. ICE was deporting Ibrahim despite the fact that he was married to a U.S. citizen and had no criminal record.

Abdulahi had good instincts for choosing whom to befriend. After his parents were murdered in Somalia, he had made it to South Africa with nothing but debt to the people who had helped him get there. Within a few years, Abdulahi had started a small shop that sold calling cards and drinks and had grown it into a success.

Abdulahi tried to maneuver his hands around the metal handcuffs to massage his wrists. If the plane was going to be grounded for some time, why didn't ICE let the passengers off the plane to walk around and stretch? It would take hours and hours until the needed part would arrive. There was plenty of time to take them off in small groups. Reaching for his shackled ankles, Abdulahi spread his knees, leaned forward as far as the waist chain would allow, and raised his feet to his hands to massage his swollen ankles. As he moved, metal dug bloody grooves into his skin. Under ICE's rules of shackling, he should have been able to fit a finger between the metal and his skin. He could not even wiggle his pinky under the metal. Weeks later, Dr. Stephen Symes of the University of Miami School of Medicine would examine the wrists and ankles of men who had been with Abdulahi on the flight. He would conclude that the scarring might be permanent.

Abdulahi examined the abrasions on his arms and legs. His heart raced. Beads of sweat gathered on his forehead. How could the United States let this happen? The United States is supposed to be a protector of human rights, not a torturer. Ibrahim threw a worried look across the aisle and tilted his head as if to say, "Hold it together." Abdulahi needed to regain control. He knew better than to ask for the cuffs to be loosened. When officers had shackled him and the others in the middle of the night at the Alexandria jail, he knew what would happen to those who complained: The officers would tighten their cuffs.

By midnight, four and a half hours after the plane landed in Senegal, it still sat motionless on the tarmac. The men and women had been shackled for over 16 hours. With the full moon, Sa'id could see uniformed men surrounding the plane, holding automatic weapons. Instead of working to release the passengers from being bound in their seats, the Senegalese airport authorities had called the police. Distant lights of the city beyond the airport taunted the imprisoned passengers, signifying the liberty that was out of their reach.

None of the men and women inside the plane were sleeping. Sa'id began to regret his decision not to get some rest the night before. When an ICE officer passed by his seat, Sa'id raised his hand as much as the cuffs would allow. "Officer," he said quickly, standing up. "Why can't we get off the plane, stretch our legs, and walk around?"

Others sitting nearby chimed in, and some also got to their feet. "We want to contact our embassy! Take off our handcuffs. We aren't animals."

Their demands multiplied. "I need my medication."

"I need to use the bathroom."

Another officer, his face hidden behind a mask, snarled, "Sit the fuck down!" The nurses who had been dispensing medication hours earlier were nowhere to be seen.

"Come with me," one of the officers ordered. "The ICE supervisor wants to talk with you." The officer was addressing Omar. Word had reached ICE about Omar's speaking for the group the night before about travel documents, at the jail. His age and fluency in both English and Somali suggested he might be a good intermediary. Without his cane, Omar hobbled to the front of the plane. Minutes passed, and then Omar's voice floated over the intercom. "Stay calm," he said in Somali. "The part for the plane is on its way. It shouldn't be too much longer." Sa'id and the other men in the back of the plane sat down. They gave Omar, and ICE, the benefit of the doubt.

Around 7 a.m., 7 hours later and almost 12 hours after the plane had landed in Dakar, light filtered through the dusty air outside the plane in a display of orange, red, and purple. The dawn brought fresh hope—dashed by distribution of breakfast. Abdulahi stared at the sandwich on the tray table in front of him. He didn't recognize the meat. He sniffed and thought it smelled old, but he was desperate to fill his stomach and welcomed any distraction. He tried to lift the sandwich to his mouth with both hands. The chains pulled his wrists back. He was forced to bow his head to close the gap between his mouth and the food. This particular indignity was nothing special. It was part of the plan—the choice ICE made in adopting its across-the-board shackling policy during transportation.

Abdulahi had tried to drink as little as possible while Flight N225AX was grounded. He wanted to avoid the bathroom. The hours dragged on. Eventually, his bladder forced him to give in. Abdulahi raised his hand. "I need to use the bathroom," he said in English. A tall SRT officer in an olive green uniform, wearing a cap and dark blue bandana to conceal his face, told Abdulahi to wait. When the officer finally motioned to him, Abdulahi staggered to his feet. Standing up in restraints was challenging under the best of circumstances. After so many hours of seated confinement, it was nearly impossible to stand, especially because Abdulahi had a leg injury from the time he was attacked by a mob in South Africa.

Abdulahi pushed against the outer limits of the shackles to anchor himself as he maneuvered out of the seat to a standing position. The chains prevented him from reaching his hands to the tops of the tan faux-leather seat backs to steady himself as he shuffled up the aisle a dozen rows toward the front of the plane. "Move it," ordered the officer, standing by the open bathroom door. Abdulahi avoided the officer's eyes as he tried to hurry, doing his best not to bump other men trying to sleep or watch a movie in the dimly lighted cabin. Arriving at the bathroom, Abdulahi squeezed by the officer to enter the small closet of a space.

He gagged at the stench. The toilet was overflowing. It had not been serviced. Feces and urine covered the floor. Abdulahi instinctively tried to cover his nose. But his chained hands could reach no higher than his chest. Exposed to the full force of the odor, Abdulahi regretted eating the sandwich for breakfast. He moved as quickly as he could, holding his breath and counting the seconds. As he struggled against the chains to unzip his pants and relieve himself, he understood why the bathroom was so foul. The shackles curtailed hand movement.

"Hurry it up," said the officer, his foot lodged in the door and his hand pushing his bandana against his nose. The officer knew how foul it was but wasn't doing anything to get it cleaned up. Abdulahi tried to wash his bound hands. Desperate to exit the bathroom, Abdulahi shuffled his way back to his seat. His legs at least were grateful for the stretch.

He and the rest of the prisoners on board had now been shackled for over 24 hours.

Morning turned to afternoon. The front door of the plane opened, letting in gusts of hot dusty air. Abdulahi caught Ibrahim's eye and glanced down the aisle. "Hey, what's happening?" An armed uniformed man strode in. A handful of others followed. They silently patrolled the aisle, their serious expressions difficult to read. Abdulahi was struck by the men's gaunt faces. The Senegalese government did not have enough money to feed its police officers. Some of the imprisoned men raised their shackles and begged for help in English or Somali, but the armed men continued down the aisle, impassive. One man near Abdulahi asked his fellow prisoners for help translating, "Does anyone speak French? We need to ask them for help, to contact our embassy, to get us off the plane!"

Abdulahi eyed the stone-faced men. He felt he had nothing to live for, no family, no future, only death and destruction. He had spent two years in ICE detention only to have his asylum case denied. He had lost contact with his wife, Fardowso, back in South Africa. He had no one left in Somalia. Abdulahi wondered what would happen if he tried to lunge for the door. Would ICE or one of the uniformed Senegalese men shoot him? A few seconds passed. Without ever looking at him, the Senegalese officers passed him and continued to the back of the plane, then crossed to the opposite aisle, making a circuit back to the front of the plane and exiting from the door they had entered. As the door closed, Abdulahi leaned back and conjured memories of his childhood in Somalia, his mother's soft words and knowing looks, his father's curious mind, and his sister's fellowship. He imagined what it would be like to reunite with his wife. These thoughts gave Abdulahi strength. He would not give in to despair, not now, not ever.

Nothing about the Senegalese police officers indicated that they were there to help, but Abdulahi pushed himself to think positive thoughts. Maybe they would permit the detained men and women to get off the plane. Or contact the United Nations or the Red Cross. But, as more minutes and hours ticked by, hope faded. Abdulahi turned to Ibrahim: "The plane isn't being fixed. No help is coming." Ibrahim reluctantly agreed.

A Senegalese news source would report, "It was not all festive at Diass the day of the inauguration of the Blaise Diagne International Airport. While the Senegalese were welcoming their new jewel, 92 of their African compatriots were tortured on the tarmac." A second news agency posed a set of rhetorical questions: "Are the Senegalese authorities aware of this incident? How is it that this ignominy is happening on our soil without anyone noticing? Why have the authorities not communicated regarding this matter?"

The men and women on ICE Air Flight N225AX had now been grounded in Dakar, immobilized in their seats, for over 20 hours, supposedly waiting for a part to arrive from the United States. They had been shackled for 12 hours more than that for a total of 32 hours. They should have been in Mogadishu, Somalia by now. How much more could they be expected to take? The toilets were inoperable, plugged with human waste. Near Sa'id, some men resorted to urinating in empty water bottles and on the floor, and on themselves. An officer, fresh off a sleep break in the first-class section of the plane, strode down the aisle. He warned: "It's a federal crime to piss in a plane."

The ventilation system was no match for the rising stink. The plane was fast becoming a latrine. Some men moaned. Others cried. A few prayed aloud.

Sa'id turned to Nadim. "The plane better start moving soon."

Just then, a man shuffled down the airplane aisle. He was wearing a security guard uniform, the clothes he had on at work when ICE arrested him. As he passed Sa'id, he said in Somali, "The plane isn't being fixed. We're stuck. I saw an officer texting 'we are going nowhere.'"

# 3  *Civil War*

## Somalia and Kenya

1991–1997

*Somalia's civil war officially began in late January 1991 when a coalition of clan militias ousted Somali dictator Siad Barre from power.*

Five-year-old Sa'id sat cross-legged on a faded blue mat made of woven plastic. It covered the dirt floor of the dugsi, the Islamic school in his neighborhood in the port city of Kismayo, Somalia. It was January 1991. The windowless, single-room school was made of vertical sticks with thinner sticks woven horizontally between them. A rusty corrugated roof sheltered students from the equatorial sun, though it leaked during seasonal rains.

In the dim light, Sa'id's bearded teacher towered over his students, all boys. He wore a white, long-sleeve shirt with his macaawiis—patterned brown fabric wrapped around his waist and draping to his shins. He held his kufi-covered head high. The single Qur'anic book in the dugsi rested open in his hands. Sa'id sat up as straight as he could to keep his collared shirt from touching his back. Yesterday, the teacher had whipped him with a tree branch for being unprepared. Today, the fabric of his shirt adhered to the wounds on his back. Sa'id listened as his teacher called on students, one at a time, to recite passages of the Qur'an in Arabic, from memory. Sa'id's heart raced and his face felt hot when the teacher rested his eyes on him and told him to stand. Sa'id got to his feet but did not speak. Every evening, after prayer, he studied the Qur'an with his parents. He needed their help because the lettering often appeared jumbled to him.

Sa'id froze. He realized he had memorized the wrong passage the previous night. The teacher's eyes narrowed. He snapped the book shut. "This time you will remember," he said. Tucking the book under his left arm, the teacher moved toward the new branch he had selected on his way to the dugsi. The branch leaned innocently against the wall. Sa'id knew that some tree branches hurt more than others. It depended on the size and suppleness of each branch.

Sa'id acted on instinct. He bolted out the door as fast as his bare feet could carry him. Outside, he ran past dusty one-story buildings with metal roofs built close together on the dry, barren land. A group of men stood at a food stand on the corner. Sa'id dodged around a woman with her baby slung on her back, then a white early-model VW van parked on the dirt road. Sa'id sped past, away from the dugsi, toward a place he knew on the edge of the developed part of the city. He had no plan. He just had to avoid another beating.

Sa'id kicked up dust as he ran. Women and children just a few years older walked by with water containers on their heads. Men led donkeys laden with bundles. Sa'id kept going, leaving behind the last cluster of thatched stick homes, reaching the undeveloped land beyond. He slowed to a walk. Trees and scrub bushes dotted the parched earth, stripped of any grass. The only sounds were baby goats bleating in the distance. He stopped and sat at the base of an acacia tree. Its feathery canopy made of thorny branches from the top of the trunk suspended small, fern-like leaves. The late morning sun sent up shimmers of dry heat off the tops of enormous termite hills that jutted out of the clay-colored land like stalagmites in a cave. Careful not to lean his sore back against the tree trunk, he caught his breath in the shade. He was alone except for two men in the distance cutting down another acacia to make charcoal and another herding half a dozen camels.

Sa'id's parents were Maryan Yusuf Ahmed and Abdi Janale Mubarak. He was the third of four children. His sister, Asha, was four years older. A year separated Sa'id from his older brother, Mohamed. Yasir was just a baby. Sa'id's family was Bajuni, an ancient people who had lived off the sea in the coastal area of Kismayo long before it became a city. The kinky hair and distinct facial features common to the Bajuni people set Sa'id and his family apart from most in Kismayo and the majority in Somalia. Most were ethnically Somali and members of particular clans. Sa'id could speak Somali and Arabic. But he also spoke the Bajuni language, Kibajuni, a dialect of Swahili.

Life was hard, but Sa'id's family fared better than many. Following Bajuni tradition, Sa'id's father and grandfather were fishermen. His grandfather owned a boat big enough to ply the coastal waters of the Indian Ocean. Sa'id's family had built their house out of tree branches covered with mud-based red plaster. Thatching covered the roof. Sa'id and his siblings slept on beds made of tightly woven dried grass with wooden legs in the main room of the two-room house, near the brightly-colored prayer rugs. His mother and sister cooked outside on three rocks over a fire. They had no electricity or running water.

As the tree's shadow grew longer, Sa'id felt the keen sting of injustice. Yet he knew it was time to go home. With heavy steps, the five-year-old made his way to his house. He arrived to find his teacher talking with his parents, who nodded as they listened. Sa'id didn't need to hear his teacher's words to know what he was saying: Sa'id had humiliated him in front of the class, encouraging disobedience. There would have to be consequences. Sa'id approached the three adults. His father turned, met his gaze, and stooped to pick up his own tree branch. Sa'id edged closer and, without a word, bent over. His father's lashes landed harder than his teacher's had the day before. Satisfied, the teacher departed. Sa'id's father spoke words

*Sa'id Abdi Janale, b. 1986, Kismayo, Somalia*
Janene Johnson, wife, m. 2015
Maryan Yusuf Ahmed, mother
Abdi Janale Mubarak, father, deceased
(Sketch by Lillian May Kew)

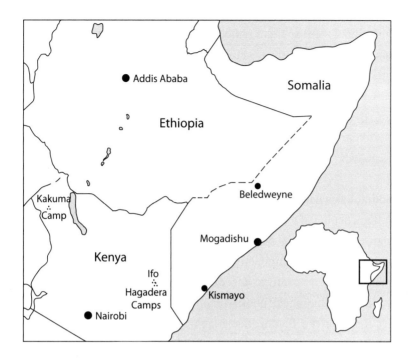

Somalia and the Hagadera, Ifo, and Kakuma refugee camps in Kenya. Courtesy of Thomas W. Sharpless.

intended to console and motivate, "It will be all right. We want you to learn. Do better."

Weeks later, Sa'id walked with his father toward a small boat launch on a beach of powdery white sand near the port of Kismayo. Sa'id held a bucket. At five years old, Sa'id was big enough to help his family on his grandfather's boat and in the fish market. Sa'id and his father headed to the family's small wooden skiff used to haul fish from his grandfather's larger fishing vessel, anchored in deeper water. Having lived his whole life near the ocean, Sa'id barely noticed the tang of brine in the air. As the port's placid, turquoise waters glistened in the bright morning sun, Sa'id noticed a small group of men in T-shirts, some of them armed, near the family's skiff. As Sa'id and his father moved closer, Sa'id realized that one of the men was his grandfather. The others shouted and pointed guns, big ones. Sa'id turned to his father and asked what the men were doing. Squinting into the sunlight, his father slowed to a halt and met his son's eyes. Abdi searched for words to explain to Sa'id that civil war had come to Kismayo.

Somalia's civil war drove out 45 percent of the Somali people, with 1.5 million fleeing to refugee camps in Kenya and beyond. Campaigns of clan-cleansing pitted neighbors and friends against each other. Violence, disease, and famine would take 500,000 lives in two years. Somalis invented a word to describe those who bore the brunt of the violence, including the poor, women, and those who lacked clan protection, like the Bajuni. Loo-maa-oyayaasha refers to "those for whom no one sheds tears over their death and destruction or to whom no one gives credit to their contributions in the making of the nation."

The civil war sprang from multiple causes, including conquest and colonialization. In the late nineteenth century, Britain, Ethiopia, and Italy seized and partitioned the land of the Somali people. Britain ruled British Somaliland in the north. Ethiopia controlled the Ogaden region, west of Somalia's current border. In the southcentral region, Italy established Italian Somaliland. After Italy's defeat in World War II, the British assumed control of Italian Somaliland and Ogaden, which Italy had invaded.

Before colonization, most Somalis were pastoralists—nomads who herded camels, sheep, and goats. Groups of people, often from the same clan, came together to pool resources and help one another. Clan affiliation, though important, was fluid and members of different clans often lived as peaceful neighbors. The colonial powers hardened clan lines. Administrators used a divide and rule approach, introducing conflicts between clans and managing the people of

Somalia as clan members rather than individuals or communities. A new class of Westernized Somali elites emerged, poised to take power once Somalia achieved independence but lacking training for their new roles. On the legacy of colonialism in Somalia, writer Imaan Daahir Saalax has observed: "The presence of colonialism still lingers today; it can be seen in the way we think, and the way we divide ourselves. We as a people have been violated on our land and in our minds."

On July 1, 1960, Somalia gained independence, and the parliamentary democracy of the Somali Republic was born. Britain drew the new nation's western border to exclude the Ogaden region, ceding it to neighboring Ethiopia, a strong ally of the United States at the time. Betrayed by its former colonizer, the newly independent Somalia looked east to the Soviet Union and China for support and protection, and guns flowed freely to Somalia's army. The militarization of Somalia had begun.

Nine years after Somalia gained independence, Siad Barre, an army general, toppled the fledgling democracy. Originally a policeman in the South of Somalia during colonial rule in the early 1940s, Barre had learned torture tactics in an Italian military school in 1950. Backed by the Soviet Union, he adopted what he called scientific socialism. Barre encouraged nationalism, literacy, and equality, and initially sought to abolish clan, class, and some gender-role distinctions. But Barre maintained control through repression and torture. In the mid-1970s, Barre's regime began to crumble after his failure to take back the Ogaden region from Ethiopia during the Ogaden War. The Soviets withdrew all aid and backed the new Marxist government of Ethiopia. The United States, seeking a new ally in the region, propped up Barre, sending years of military aid that allowed him to cling onto power through the end of the Cold War. By the late 1980s, the world's two superpowers had armed Somalia to the teeth, making it the most militarized nation in Africa.

Weakened by his defeat in the Ogaden War, in 1978 Barre abandoned his push for a unified Somali identity and instead bred distrust among clans, keeping his enemies fractured and waging a war of terror that killed or imprisoned tens of thousands of his own people. As Cold War tensions subsided, the United States no longer needed Barre as an ally. In 1990, the United States withdrew aid to Somalia and started calling Barre a human rights violator. Full-scale civil war broke out in late January 1991, when clan-based militias from the north and south allied to oust Barre from power. The south and central areas of Somalia—including Sa'id's hometown of Kismayo—were ground zero for the war between clan militias seeking to control territory and resources. After Barre fled Mogadishu, the United Somali Congress, the Hawiye clan militia that helped to overthrow Barre, started fighting Barre's clan militias in Kismayo and took control in April 1991.

On the Kismayo beach near his family's skiff, Sa'id listened as the men pointed guns at his grandfather. "They are taking the fishing boat," explained his father, who put his hand on Sa'id's shoulder and turned him around, away from the threatening men and back up the beach path. The hijacking was part of the violence and pillaging of the newly erupted civil war. There was nothing they could do to help Sa'id's grandfather. A religious man who never carried a gun, the elderly fisherman didn't stand a chance. As Sa'id walked away with his father in silence, a stiff offshore breeze kicked up whitecaps on the water. Sa'id looked back. The disappearing figure of his grandfather still gestured with the men. That was the last time Sa'id would ever see his grandfather.

A few days later, Sa'id sat in school at the dugsi. Outside, clan militia vehicles with mounted machine guns rolled down nearby dirt roads. Men in fatigues and dark glasses carried automatic weapons, their chests crisscrossed with bandoliers of ammunition. As the militia neared the school, the soldiers opened fire. Bullets tore through the stick walls of the school as if they were paper. As the rhythmic popping surrounded Sa'id, his teacher dropped the Qur'anic book and shouted for his students to lie down. Some of the children obeyed while others just crumpled to the floor. The bullets kept coming—through the wall facing the street, from unseen shooters outside. Wounded children cried out for their mothers. Sa'id's teacher was dead. So were the boys Sa'id had played with just that morning before school. Next to Sa'id lay the motionless body of the boy who, seconds earlier, had been standing to recite the day's Qur'an passages. Sa'id held himself perfectly still.

After minutes that felt like hours, the "pop, pop, pop" of gunshots moved on, down the street, away from the school. By some miracle, Sa'id had escaped death. He raised his head. Only one other boy, across the room, had survived. They locked eyes and crawled across the bodies of their classmates and out the back of the dugsi. They silently separated, heading for home as fast as they could.

As he ran, Sa'id looked around in disbelief. The militia had mowed people down everywhere. Men, women, and children who had just been walking and talking now lay on the ground in pools of their own blood. Infants screamed, still strapped to the backs of their mothers. More gunshots rang out, but now in the distance. A haze of dust from the military vehicles, combined with smoke from gunfire, hung in the air. Sa'id's sobs were punctuated with coughing. His bare feet were stained red by the bloodied earth as he ran. Sa'id was 5, but he ran as fast as if he were 15, dashing through the door of his house, into his mother Maryan's arms. She held him tight, rocking him back and forth, holding prayer beads, and whispering words meant to soothe him. She told him not to worry, that Allah would help them, that it would be okay. But her trembling arms conveyed a different message.

In the days that followed, armed men roamed the streets at all hours. Sa'id's family huddled in their house, venturing out only to find food. In a city of over half a million, Sa'id's people numbered only a few thousand. Because the Bajuni had no militia of their own, it was only a matter of time before enemy gunmen would show up in the Bajuni part of the city and at Sa'id's house.

It happened at night, swiftly and without warning. Sa'id, his parents, his older brother Mohamed, his sister Asha, and his baby brother Yasir were together, in the main room of their house. They had no guns or other means of defense. Armed men burst through the door. Within seconds, the men shot Sa'id's father in the head. He slumped to the floor within a few feet of Sa'id. The child watched as his father's blood spilled in front of him. The men turned to Maryan, who clutched baby Yasir and told her older children to run. The men would take her away to rape her.

Sa'id felt Mohamed's shaking hands on his shoulders, steering him out the back of the house. Running and sobbing, the three young children escaped to the house of a neighbor. Days would pass before Maryan found her children. She and Yasir had survived, but her face was etched with an enduring grief. Through tears that would flow for years, she told her children they were going to Kenya. Her sister was married to a man with an 18-wheeler truck. He would drive them.

Sa'id, his mother, and his siblings walked for hours to get to the truck. With gunfire in the distance, they passed bodies along the side of the road. Finally in the flatbed of the 18-wheeler, the family huddled together with dozens of people fleeing the massacres, packed in as tight as bags of rice. They drove, bribing their way through clan militia roadblocks. Sa'id felt every rock, dip, and turn of the truck. He did his best to block out the wails of injured and dying people around him in the truck. The smell of diesel mixed with the stench of blood, sweat, and death. Sa'id wished the truck would stop so that those still living could remove the dead. But the truck kept on through the night.

The militia fighting made it impossible to travel by land to Kenya, so Sa'id's uncle drove the truck south, down the coast to a boat. The boat ferried them to a port on the northern coast of Kenya. From there, Kenyan authorities transported them to Camp Hagadera, newly established for civil war refugees. It would become part of the sprawling Dadaab group of camps run by the United Nations High Commissioner for Refugees (UNHCR), the international organization founded to aid refugees around the world. Its guiding principles were set by the 1951 United Nations Convention relating to the Status of Refugees and its 1967 Protocol.

Nothing but sand and thorn bushes stretched as far as Sa'id could see. The family waited in a line with other survivors—a hostile sun beating down on them—until a Kenyan man motioned to Sa'id's mother and gave her a small tent and some food from a truck. Sa'id examined the tent and wondered how the whole family would fit. The food supplies were a bag of flour, a bag of rice, oil, and half a leg of goat. It was meant to last the family of five a month. Hunger loomed, but they were alive.

Preparing and preserving the meat ration to last, without refrigeration, became a ritual of survival. Sa'id watched as his mother, with surgical precision, cut the meat off the bone into thin strips that she sun-dried and then cooked, minced, and stored in ghee, a preservation method called muqmad. Meals consisted of one spoonful of meat with rice. Once, Sa'id asked for a second helping. "No, my son. I know that you are hungry, but we need to make the meat last," his mother explained. He never asked again.

Day after day, the heat rose off the land in waves of hot haze. One time a wind came up. Strong gusts caught the kite-thin walls of the tent, tugging the shelter in fits and starts, up and across the dirt, away toward the horizon. Sa'id and Mohamed started running after the tent. It seemed to taunt them—slowing until the boys almost reached it and then speeding up, evading their grasp. They needed to catch it; failure was not an option. There was no place where they could get another tent. The boys ran as if their life depended on it, until finally they caught up to the tent and dragged it back to their mother, desperate to stop her tears.

One night, some weeks later, Sa'id woke up because it sounded like someone was in the tent. Terrified and unsure, he did nothing. The next morning, Sa'id's mother was making malawah, Somali breakfast pancakes, when she realized the meat was missing. For the rest of the month, the family ate only rice with sugar for dinner, and every night, Sa'id's mother cried herself to sleep. Sa'id blamed himself for becoming an accomplice to his siblings' hunger and his mother's grief.

By the time Sa'id was six, in 1992, the family had moved to Camp Ifo. Also part of the Dadaab camp, Ifo had just opened, and the land had not yet been cleared of trees. Lines of tents were just beginning to form over the vast land. The Dadaab group of camps would eventually shelter close to half a million people and cover 15 square miles. Sa'id's family was given a new tent, bigger and more permanent than the one Sa'id and Mohamed had chased across the sand.

Better shelter did not alter the reality of their life—reduced to waiting and the barest acts of survival. Sa'id and his family longed for messages from other relatives forced out by the war and waited for word on their family application for refugee status. If Sa'id and his family were found to be refugees, they could be relocated to another country, but only if that country agreed to accept them.

Three years would drag by before Sa'id's mother's name appeared on a paper tacked to the wall of Ifo's medical clinic—the list of people who could take the next step toward refugee status. This next step meant another move, to Camp Kakuma, a two-day drive away, in the remote reaches of northwest Kenya.

The UNHCR established Camp Kakuma in 1992 to protect thousands of unaccompanied South Sudanese children who were fleeing war near the Sudan-Kenya border, the so-called Lost Boys. By the time Sa'id's family arrived at the camp in 1995, its population was approaching 50,000. Over the next 10 years, the camp's numbers would swell to almost 200,000 and include people not only from South Sudan and Somalia but also Ethiopia, Uganda, Burundi, and Congo. Like other refugee camps, Kakuma packed its residents into close quarters. People made do, constructing shelters from thorn branches, mud, and tarps, or making mud bricks to build huts with tin roofs. Safety was a constant concern. Each year brought hundreds of reports of burglaries, assaults, and sexual violence in the camp. Sa'id sometimes awoke at night to gunshots, the sound stirring up memories of Somalia.

Camp Kakuma, like the other camps, had no running water, sanitation, or electricity. Its residents suffered from malnutrition, lack of hygiene, and diseases like cholera. The arid land, dotted with termite hills, frequently reached 115 degrees Fahrenheit. When intense seasonal rains arrived, the water quickly filled the parched land of two nearby dry riverbeds, sometimes flooding the camp. Mosquito-infested pools of standing water were left where residents extracted mud for bricks, making malaria a threat. Newcomers were cautioned to watch out for cobras, scorpions, and venomous spiders. There was never enough food or water, and the water that was available was dirty and had bugs in it. Sa'id, skinny, with protruding ribs, contracted tapeworms and a parasite camp residents called the DooDoo bug, which burrowed into his skin under his toenails. Getting water was a daily ordeal. Sometimes hundreds of people would wait in line for water. It was Sa'id's job to join the queue with a plastic five-gallon jug that, once filled by the single spigot, he would carry on his head back to his family.

Sa'id and his family had hoped their stay in Kakuma would be short, another way station along the long road toward the place where they would build their new life. But months passed, and then years. The temporary camps grew into an established community with an economy of shops and services. A main street formed, and a market, even a local art scene. Kakuma morphed into a sprawling refugee city, about 10 miles wide.

Camp Kakuma was located in the poorest region of Kenya, near the land of the Turkana people. They were pastoralists who, like many Somalis, followed the seasonal grazing patterns with their animals. Their long necks adorned with beads, their big guns, and their shoes made from tires all made an impression on Sa'id. Other Somali refugees talked about the Turkana as a skilled and fierce people who sometimes clashed among themselves over cattle and boundaries for grazing. Fortunately, the refugees in Kakuma and the host Turkana community coexisted in peace, for the most part.

A few months into their stay at Camp Kakuma, Sa'id and his brother Mohamed decided to play soccer with some other boys. It was hot enough to cook meat on a rock, so the boys were waiting until the heat of the day passed. As the sun lowered, they walked, barefoot in the dry clay soil, to the outskirts of the camp, weaving through low thorny bushes. The boys would kick off their game in the dry riverbed, the only place clear enough of scrub brush for soccer.

Sa'id led the group through bushes with thorns draped with old plastic bags that desert winds had blown from the camp. All of a sudden, he stopped short. There, in front of him, tucked under the branches, was a small, still figure. He said a short prayer. The other boys silently crowded behind him. Sa'id couldn't take his eyes off the baby. Not even one year old, the child was missing an arm and a leg. With her sunburned skin, she looked as if she had been roasted. Abandoning any thought of soccer, Sa'id and the other boys ran back to the camp, where his baby brother was safe.

No one went to bury the baby for hours, not until after midnight. Sa'id couldn't stop crying, for the baby and for himself. He felt just as expendable.

The UNHCR administered Kakuma from a compound of air-conditioned, concrete buildings, arranged in a square and securely fenced off from the rest of the camp. From their cool offices, camp officials imposed head counts and rules, like the prohibition on leaving to seek employment. Every day, Sa'id and his mother walked to a bulletin board outside a UNHCR office to check if their names appeared on a list showing they had been accepted for resettlement abroad. Sa'id watched people who had arrived at the camp after them make the list first. "Be patient, my son," his mother told him—her steady resolve transforming the daily routine into a ritual of hope.

At long last, in 1997, their names appeared on the list. Sa'id was 11. After six years in the camps, Sa'id and his family received refugee status and could look forward to resettlement in the United States. Sa'id's mother had started a new relationship during those long years, with Abdi Yusef. She and Abdi had two children, a daughter, Rema, and a son, Noor. Abdi would not be allowed to travel with the family to the United States though. Sa'id's mother had been in line for refugee status before her relationship with Abdi, and her place in line was connected to her status as the female head of a family. Joining Abdi to her application would result in the family losing its place in line. Sa'id's stepfather would not reunite with the family until 2008, 11 years later.

A few months after his family's names appeared on the list, Sa'id sat in the window seat of a jumbo jet headed for Dallas, Texas. The pilot announced that they would be landing in 15 minutes. Sa'id peeked out the window, down at the vast, flat land dominated by impossibly tall buildings of glass and steel. Cars streamed down three-lane highways leading to the center of the city, like spokes of a wheel. He marveled at what he had only imagined. Gone was a life of endless waiting in a hot, barren land, on the edge of starvation, a tent the only relief from the fierce sun and a daily list of names the only source of hope. Sa'id was about to touch down in a world of running water, flush toilets, pillowy beds, television, air conditioning, and packaged foods of endless variety—and, he thought, safety and opportunity.

Everything gleamed inside the Dallas airport. The floors, the shops, even the bathrooms sparkled with a newness and permanency Sa'id had never experienced. Everyone walked as if they were late for something important. But Sa'id and his family, unsure and overwhelmed, moved slowly, his mother clutching an International Office of Migration bag, white with blue lettering: IOM. People hurried past, without so much as a glance.

Sa'id and his family approached a group standing and waiting, some holding signs with names scrawled across them. A White family of three held two signs, reading "Ahmed" and "Maryan." Maryan Ahmed, his mother's name. The White family smiled. Sa'id smiled back, thinking that they really did not need the signs. His family's ragged clothes, bewildered expressions, and IOM bag telegraphed who they were. The Dallas family were church volunteers, assigned to help Sa'id's family transition into American society. The first stop was a two-bedroom hotel suite and then a grocery store. The array of vegetables and fruits, all fresh and cool, dazzled Sa'id.

Amid such bounty, the reality of Sa'id's new life soon set in. Sa'id's mother now had 6 children to support, aged 1 to 15. She worked two jobs at warehouses, leaving the house early in the morning, returning late at night. After she returned home from her second job, she cooked food that the older children would heat up for dinner the next evening. This unforgiving schedule left almost no time for parenting. Maryan worried the entire time she worked. She was afraid the children might burn the apartment down. She knew her neighborhood was not safe. The family's home had already been burglarized, and the kids stepped over empty beer bottles and used needles on their way to the school bus stop. America was a dream come true, but Sa'id's mother still cried every night, just as she had done in the refugee camps.

Sa'id began attending Preston Hollow Elementary School in Dallas. He had only been in fifth grade for a few months when he found himself perched on a hard wooden chair in the principal's office, shaking and confused. The White man behind the desk spoke to Sa'id in words he did not fully understand. A teacher had sent Sa'id to the principal for saying something he had heard on television. Sa'id didn't know the meaning of the words he had repeated. He thought he was cracking a joke, but the teacher had not been amused.

The principal rose, approached Sa'id, and motioned for him to stand behind the chair with his hands resting on its back. Turning on his heels, the principal walked a few steps to a closet where he kept a broad wooden paddle. Having been flogged many times in Somalia, Sa'id knew what was coming. He tensed up, stifling his cries, as the man swung hard, putting his full weight behind the paddle strikes.

Corporal punishment was legal in Texas in 1997 and remains legal in some states today. In 1977, the Supreme Court heard a case, *Ingraham v. Wright*, in which a teacher had hit one boy so severely that he required medical attention and could not return to school for three days. The Supreme Court nevertheless ruled that corporal punishment in school does not violate the Constitution, leaving states to decide whether to allow it or not. Some states, like Texas, chose to permit it, even though statistics showed that teachers were using physical punishment disproportionately against Black students. Three years after Sa'id first sat in the principal's office, in 2000, Texas school teachers and officials would paddle 73,994 students, the most in the country.

At home that night, Sa'id's mother tried to reduce the swelling of his wounds with ice, but Sa'id could not sit comfortably for three days. He concluded, "Here they also whip kids, and they use bigger paddles."

Sa'id soon learned that the school principal would not be the only source of violence in his new life. Sa'id's secondhand clothes and limited English made him an easy target for school bullies. Each day brought a new round of insults and beatings from other children. "African booty scratcher!" was the usual slur, followed by a shove or a fist in the face.

"I did not raise you to run away," said his mother, as she tended to his bruises each night. "Never start a fight. But if they raise a hand, you must defend yourself."

One morning, at the school-bus stop, Sa'id took his mother's advice. When some boys pushed Sa'id and ripped his backpack, he fought back. After Sa'id used his fists, the boys never touched him again. Staying safe, and gaining respect, meant fighting violence with violence.

Sa'id had begun to adapt to life in the United States.

# 4  *Shiqaal Subclan*

Beledwyne, Somalia

2005

*Clans are kinship groups based on paternal bloodlines that have formed the basis of social organization in Somalia for over a thousand years, with the Hawiye as a major clan and Shiqaal as one of its subclans.*

Abdulahi thrashed his arms and legs in the swift river current. By trial and error, he learned which frantic motions would keep him afloat and moving. The 18-year-old had tied empty plastic bottles around his waist as a makeshift float. The bottles interfered with his strokes, but he hesitated to remove them. Abdulahi was teaching himself to swim in the Shabelle River, a beast of a waterway that snaked through his hometown of Beledwyne, Somalia. The river regularly flooded its banks, inundating the city's flat land. Unlike the desert areas of the rest of Somalia, the southcentral region near the Shabelle and Jubba rivers contains a fertile valley that can sustain crops, like cowpeas and corn.

By teaching himself to swim, Abdulahi defied his parents. "There are crocodiles. People have lost their lives," his mother always warned. Abdulahi pretended to capitulate. A good son did as he was told, and Abdulahi wanted to be a good son. But some force propelled Abdulahi to teach himself to swim, even though Beledwyne—unlike the coastal capital city of Mogadishu, 200 miles away—was landlocked, and the only swimmable body of water in his hometown was the treacherous Shabelle. With a population of over 300,000, Beledwyne is the fifth largest city in Somalia, on the border with Ethiopia and along a main route to Mogadishu. A sprawl of buildings, mostly one- or two-stories, covered 20 square miles of dusty flat land, crisscrossed by dirt roads. Beledwyne had been an Italian colony, and Italy's influence was still visible in the vestiges of neo-classical architecture—and the ubiquity of pasta.

Abdulahi focused on the far bank of the Shabelle. After five minutes of vigorous thrashing, he touched bottom and dragged himself up onto the bank of packed dirt spotted with thorny shrubs. His T-shirt and loose pants clung to his skinny limbs. He raised his arms in victory before collapsing to catch his breath.

The sun cast orange and yellow light over the low concrete buildings of the city. Abdulahi fought the current once more back to his side of town. He dropped the bottles and rope where he had found them by the side of the bank and, barefoot, ran the mile to his family's home in the center of town. He hoped his clothes would dry before he got home. Abdulahi had disobeyed his parents, but he'd rather not lie.

Abdulahi's path home took him past his mother's one-room shop—selling dry goods and other home essentials, now shuttered for the day—and down Beledwyne's main street to the center of town. People bustled along the dusty street, flanked by concrete block buildings, mainly storefronts, painted in vibrant hues of red, yellow, and blue. The non-pedestrian traffic consisted of a handful of cars and donkey-drawn carriages, still common in twenty-first century Beledwyne. As Abdulahi approached his family's house, he slowed to a walk and nodded to his next-door neighbor, a man in his early 50s with a long gray beard and lines from the sun on his face.

Abdulahi's family home was typical for the area—stick walls lashed together and plastered white with a mix of cow manure and sand, the roof corrugated metal, and the floor smooth packed dirt. Dried corn stalks hung off the house provided shade in back, where his mother and sister were cooking. It was not much. But it was home. Abdulahi stepped inside.

Abdulahi's mother, Maryam Abdulle Adow, crouched in the middle of the backyard, stirring an iron pot perched on rocks over the open fire. Firewood was stacked near the side of the house. A wire fence enclosed the small dirt area. Maryam wore a light-blue skirt and a tan long-sleeve blouse, with a maroon head scarf that outlined her face and draped to her shoulders. Hearing her son, Maryam called out over her shoulder, "Your father is at the mosque. He will be home soon."

Abdulahi's family were Sufi Muslims. Sufism is an ancient sect of Islam common throughout Somalia. Weekly Sufi rituals involve chanting, rhythmic swaying, and the reading of poetry to reach a transcendent, sometimes trance-like state, often at the tombs of deceased saints. Sufis stressed the importance of inner life through meditation, seclusion, and self-denial. Compared to other strands of Islam, Sufis have a reputation for loving music and being less political than other Muslims. They have endured destruction and desecration of their shrines by more orthodox, often young, Muslims influenced by Arab countries. Later, in 2008, Sufis in Beledwyne would arm themselves to fight al-Shabaab, forcing the militant group out of the city.

Abdulahi's sister, Hamdi, was helping their mother cook. Four years younger than Abdulahi, Hamdi did not share her brother's love of outdoor adventures. Instead, she could be found most often by their mother's side. She resembled their father—tall and dark. Her behavior also mirrored their father's; Hamdi was bookish and disciplined in her habits. Most Somali parents understood the importance of education, but not all of them made the education of their daughters a priority. Luckily for Hamdi, she and Abdulahi both attended private school. She tackled her studies with an earnestness that Abdulahi found hard to muster.

As Abdulahi stood in the open doorway facing the backyard where his mother and sister were cooking, Hamdi looked up. She saw in a flash that her brother had been swimming. Although she curled the edges of her mouth, the look in her eyes assured Abdulahi she would not betray him. Abdulahi grinned back and promised himself he would return the favor. Each was the other's keeper, despite their age difference.

Maryam glanced over her shoulder as she continued speaking to Abdulahi, "The boys stopped by, asking for you to play soccer tomorrow." Soccer was what Abdulahi loved most in life.

"Yes, it's a big game. We're renting a good ball." Abdulahi turned and went back inside to wait for his father.

Abdulahi's mother, like so many Somalis, had lived a life touched deeply by loss. The civil war in the early 1990s took her brother. Maryam's father had passed away a short time after. When Abdulahi was a small child, her sister died giving birth in the family's house. Through all of this tragedy, Maryam moved forward, determined to lift up both her young family and her community. When the local Red Cross offered a medical course in childbirth, she trained as a midwife, seeking to ensure that other women would not die as her sister had. With her two children, Maryam stressed the importance of education and did everything in her power to help them navigate the dangers of their clan-based society.

Those dangers were extreme. Despite the fact that Somalia had established a fledgling democracy after gaining independence in 1960, during Maryam's lifetime the country had devolved into the strongman government of Siad Barre and then further disintegrated into militarized clan factionalism. With no central government, the country was run by a patchwork system of rule by clans and

*Abdulahi Hassan Mohumed, b. 1985, Beledwyne, Somalia*
Ifraah Abdi Ali, wife, m. 2009, deceased
Fardowso Ahmed Abdi, wife, m. 2015
Maryam Abdulle Adow, mother, deceased
Hassan Mohumed Garad, father, deceased
Hamdi Hassan Mohumed, sister
(Sketch by Malcolm Stanton)

subclans—kinship groups defined by patrilineal bloodlines. The major clans of Somalia included the Hawiye, Dir, Darod, Isaaq, Digil, and Mirifle.

Most, but not all, Somalis are members of a clan and trace their genealogy to a set of common ancestors, a group of six Arab founders believed to be descended from the prophet Mohammed. From the time they are toddlers, children are taught to recite their paternal lineage back multiple generations. Male Somali names reflect the clan structure—composed of a given name, followed by the names of the person's father, grandfather, and great-grandfather. Abdulahi's name going back three generations is Abdulahi Hassan Mohumed Garad, which reflects the first names of his father, Hassan, his grandfather, Mohumed, and his great-grandfather, Garad.

In Abdulahi's home city of Beledwyne, a subclan of the Hawiya major clan—the Hawadle—dominated. Most people living in Beledwyne were Hawadle. Being Hawadle meant increased access to all forms of opportunity, from lower prices for food to increased marital prospects and better jobs. Being Hawadle also bestowed protection, as there was no police force. Not everyone in Beledwyne was Hawadle or even a member of another clan, however. Maryam's family had no clan but instead belonged to a caste, the Madhiban, also known as the Midgan. The Madhiban did not trace their ancestry to a major clan. Rather, they were an occupational caste of Somali people who were traditionally "hunters, shoemakers, tanners, well diggers and water carriers for their hosts." Considered "dirty" by the Somali majority, Madhiban occupied the lower echelon of Somali society and faced not only stigma and discrimination, but also physical violence at the hands of the most powerful clans. Maryam's family did not engage in the traditional Madhiban occupations but owned a small shop that sold imported goods like rice, sugar, salt, and soap. It was at this shop that Maryam's path crossed with that of Abdulahi's father, Hassan Mohumed Garad.

Tall, lanky, and clean-shaven, Hassan dressed like many Somali men, in trousers and long-sleeved, button-down shirts. But his minority status was obvious because Hassan was what Somalis call "hard hair" or jareer. The majority of Somalis consider themselves jileec and have thin curly hair, or "soft hair." Hassan's hair was kinky, like that of many from other parts of Africa. He was not a member of his wife's Madhiban caste but was Shiqaal. Like the Hawadle, the Shiqaal was a subclan of the Hawiye, but unlike the Hawadle, the Shiqaal subclan was small and lacked power.

Somalis like Hassan, whose ancestors hailed from other African nations rather than the Middle East, are often descendants of enslaved people. In the eighteenth century, the slave trade brought people to southcentral Somalia and forced them to work on plantations in its fertile valley. To call someone jareer or "hard hair" is to invoke this history. When slavery was abolished in the mid-twentieth century, freed people adopted the clan of their former owners or joined other clans for protection and identity. Hassan's membership in the Shiqaal clan was thus not by blood, but by affiliation, and his ancestry of being descended from enslaved people carried a stigma. Hassan thus had two counts against him: his clan, the Shiqaal, which was small and weak, and his "hard hair."

Despite these societal disadvantages, Hassan did not hesitate to pursue Maryam. He made excuses to visit her family's shop, and their mutual affection grew, even though Maryam's family objected to the match. Maryam was committed to marry someone else, someone approved of by her family, someone who was also Madhiban. It was taboo for Maryam to marry outside her caste. Only when Maryam became pregnant with Abdulahi did her parents relent.

Abdulahi had been home from swimming less than an hour when Hassan swung open the door, ready for dinner with his wife and children. His booming voice filled the house. Abdulahi emerged from a back room and smiled a greeting to his father as he headed outside to wash his hands before eating. Although Hamdi took after their father more than he did, Abdulahi revered Hassan, and the two shared a close bond. Hassan had risen above his circumstances, and Abdulahi aspired to do the same.

The family gathered in the main room of the house. Maryam and Hamdi set out four plates, placing the meal they had cooked on a circular platter at the center of the table. Hassan and Abdulahi seated themselves across from each other, as did Maryam and Hamdi. They gathered for dinner almost every day, but it still felt special—the one time they could count on to be together, just the four of them. Hassan and Maryam started to talk about what was running low at the store. As Abdulahi's mother shared her plans for restocking the sugar supply, Abdulahi reached for his favorite dish piled high on the platter—surbiyaan hilib adhi, a rice-based goat dish with raisins and onions, seasoned with saffron. He helped himself to a folded piece of canjeero, a close cousin to Ethiopian injera—the spongy flat bread used instead of utensils, and dug in. Once everyone was eating, Hassan cleared his throat and regarded his two children before measuring his words. "Your mother and I think it's time we told you something." He paused and then continued, "I've received a request from the Hawadle clan militia. They want me to leave my job." Abdulahi stopped eating. He knew it was serious when the Hawadle were involved.

Abdulahi's father was a teacher of English and math. Months earlier, Hassan had left his previous position because the school administrators were underpaying him due to his minority clan status. He found a new position at a school where the owner not only paid him the salary he deserved but also took an interest in Abdulahi's education, encouraging him to apply for scholarships that would allow the young adult to study abroad.

"Why don't they want you working at the Universal Private School?" Abdulahi asked when he found his voice. Hamdi looked down at her plate. No one was eating.

"It has to do with influence," his father said. "They think I reach more people at this job than my old one. They don't want me teaching so many people."

"What are you going to do?" Abdulahi already knew the answer.

Hassan looked at Maryam and then back to Abdulahi. "I have to resign. It would be too dangerous not to."

After dinner, Hassan retired to the spare room he used as an office. There, he kept his prized possessions, including a journal in which he noted important events. Because of their father's meticulous record-keeping, Abdulahi and Hamdi knew their true dates of birth, unlike many Somalis. For most in Somalia, birthdates hold little meaning, and birth certificates are rare. Somalis are more likely to commemorate anniversaries of the passing of loved ones than to celebrate birthdays.

Hassan also kept books in English in his home office. English held endless fascination for him. At restaurants, he would read the scraps of English-language newspapers that were cut up for use as napkins. Once, when Abdulahi told his father that he would rather learn Arabic than English, his father admonished him: "If you learn Arabic, you can talk with people from a few other countries. If you learn English, you can communicate with the world." But Abdulahi would never learn English from his father. He would gain that skill only later, while he was in immigration detention in the United States.

Hassan had learned English after being kidnapped into the army of strongman Siad Barre as a young teen during the 1970s. Gun-toting men plucked him from a nomadic life and plunged him into a daily routine of washing the shoes and laundry of soldiers in Beledwyne. At the time, Somalia was at war with Ethiopia over Ogaden, the large expanse of disputed territory just to the west of Beledwyne.

The Ogaden War started in 1977, lasted nine months, and killed over a third of the Somali army. Although Hassan had not actively fought while in the army, he had seen enough to caution his son: "Stay out of the military if you can. They will force you into war for nothing."

After Hassan's military service came to an end, he began working days as an assistant to a bus driver, collecting bus fares. At night, for the first time in his life, he attended school. Intelligent and eager for an education, Hassan quickly learned how to read and write in Somali. Within a few years, he mastered a working proficiency in English as well as Italian.

Now, at home, in his office, Hassan lit a candle to read by. He selected a volume about Somalia's colonial history. Abdulahi, his belly full of his mother's cooking, headed for bed, weary from his exertions on the river and his father's news. He was soon asleep.

The next day, Abdulahi raced down the center of the soccer field, toward the ball. He was at the open-air field at the edge of Beledwyne, where youth teams played one another. Today was the big game against his team's archrival. A kick from the goalie of Abdulahi's team had sent the rented ball deep into the other team's territory. Sweat drenched Abdulahi's white T-shirt, spray-painted with the name of his soccer team, as he raced toward the ball. Dusty clods kicked out behind him as his bare feet dug into the dry bare ground. Small scars from the toenails of other players pocked his shins, trophies of past games. He hoped that the cloth knotted around his waist that he wore instead of shorts wouldn't come loose during the all-out dash. The teams were tied, with only a few minutes left on the clock. Abdulahi had already scored one goal.

Two defenders from the other team responded to Abdulahi's threat, but Abdulahi reached the ball first. He looked up. He was close to the goal, but he had to get past the two players barreling toward him. The first arrived with a body check—a foul that would not halt the play, as there was no referee. Abdulahi kept moving forward through the impact, turning a few degrees at the moment of contact to protect the ball. The collision with the defender sent him airborne for a moment, but the ball remained close to his feet. Faking a turn left, he went right and passed the ball to a teammate who had been left undefended. Abdulahi pressed forward, overtaking the second defender. He was free to receive the ball back. It came, as expected. Now it was just him and the goalie, who had moved toward him to block the shot. But Abdulahi only needed a small opening. He chose the right top corner of the goal and sent the ball there. The goalie didn't stand a chance. His team had won.

Abdulahi slowed to a stop, his mouth broadening into a smile. Hands on his bent knees, he caught his breath. He looked up at the opposing goalie, a few yards away, trying to read his face. Best to be careful. Sometimes, scoring too much prompted boys from the other team to attack him.

Abdulahi could hear his teammates rallying behind him, "Great job, Shiqaal!" They were Hawadle boys. They appreciated his skill but refused to use his name, instead calling him the name of his clan. His teammates would likely defend him if the opposing team started something. They had always stuck up for him in the past, but Abdulahi could never be sure if the next time would be different.

Clan hierarchy infused all aspects of life in Beledwyne. Everyone knew each other's clan affiliation; it was part of personal identity. With no functioning government in Somalia, kinship connections undergird social and economic networks as well as political life. As a young person, Abdulahi's principal experience of the clan structure was verbal bullying that could escalate into physical violence. Every day at school, Hawadle boys surrounded him, hurling insults at "Shiqaal." On the worst days, these encounters ended with the other boys beating on Abdulahi. Worried for her son, his mother would give him money to take Hawadle boys to the movies. But such protection money had little effect at school. In a society organized around group affiliations, Abdulahi and his family had few to turn to for help.

The opposing goalie ignored Abdulahi, letting him savor victory with his teammates before heading home. He was happiest on the soccer field. It was the one place where people recognized his skill, not simply his clan.

Two weeks after the Hawadle clan threat, Abdulahi's father resigned from his teaching position, leaving Maryam's small shop as the family's only source of income. Reluctantly, Abdulahi's parents decided that Hassan must also sacrifice his home office so they could rent out the spare room. The only tenant they could find was a Hawadle man named Ali Qanyare—the tall, proud, and gun-toting brother of a Hawadle military leader.

For several months, all seemed well with this arrangement. Abdulahi's father was looking for a new job, while his mother tended the store. Ali Qanyare's rent money helped make ends meet. But the relative calm was not to last. Ali Qanyare stopped paying rent. Next, he demanded that Abdulahi's parents sell him the house. He liked the location in the center of town. Emboldened by the backing of his brother's militia, Ali Qanyare was used to getting what he wanted. But Abdulahi's parents resisted. Hassan had built the home, and Maryam had given birth to both children within its walls. Other than the small store, the house was all the family had.

In the absence of any functioning governmental authority, Abdulahi's parents followed tradition to resolve the conflict: They asked the Hawadle elders to intercede. But the elders were unable to exert influence over Ali Qanyare. The clan militias had become too powerful, a law unto themselves. He continued to demand the house. When Abdulahi's parents refused to give in, Ali Qanyare resorted to other means.

Abdulahi and his sister were home alone the evening Ali Qanyare's men burst in, guns drawn. They grabbed Abdulahi and Hamdi, forcing them into two military cars. When Abdulahi struggled, the men beat him with the butts of their guns before pulling hoods over the siblings' heads. The kidnappers drove Abdulahi and Hamdi to a remote house and separated them. The kidnappers then tied Abdulahi to a tree and thrashed him with sticks. At the sound of Hamdi's distant screams, Abdulahi felt he could bear any beating, any level of pain if it would save his sister from being raped. But there was no bargain to save his 14-year-old sister from the men.

Abdulahi's parents pleaded in vain with Ali Qanyare for their children's release. Finally, after three days, they succeeded in negotiating a ransom for Abdulahi and Hamdi's release. Abdulahi and Hamdi returned to their parents, but the trauma remained. Abdulahi would never forget the cries and sobs of his sister or the feeling of being at the mercy of people who could kill you in an instant.

The ransom, though substantial, bought only a temporary reprieve. Ali Qanyare would not rest until he had their house. Abdulahi's parents had no choice but to agree to the forced sale. In October of 2005, Hassan set a meeting with Ali Qanyare to exchange the title documents for payment. Abdulahi bristled at the injustice but took some comfort in the idea that selling the house would end the conflict with Ali Qanyare.

On the day of the meeting, Abdulahi's parents waited at the house in nervous anticipation, preparing for their transaction with Ali Qanyare. Hamdi was in a back room of the house while Abdulahi tended his mother's store a short distance away. Customers, women known to Abdulahi, stepped in from the street to negotiate prices for rice, soap, and salt. The store was open to the street; when closed, it was secured by metal shutters and a padlock. Racks of shelf-stable food items lined the walls. Bags of wheat flour and rice crowded the worn cement floor. As Abdulahi was helping a customer, Hamdi appeared, her shoulders heaving as she sobbed. "They stabbed father and shot mother!" she said, clinging to her brother. "They are both dead." Hamdi had narrowly escaped by running out the back door of the house.

Abdulahi knew instantly that the men would come after him next, to eliminate any future threat to the title to the property. Their black cars were already approaching.

Hamdi's crying had attracted the attention of Farah Osman, the landlord of the family's shop. Farah beckoned the siblings to follow him out the back of the store to his house, just steps away. They were just in time. Ali Qanyare's men arrived at the shop to find no one. Abdulahi and Hamdi were safe for the moment, but Abdulahi could not stop shaking, in anger and terror.

Staying more than one night at Farah's house, so close to the shop, would be too dangerous for Abdulahi, the male heir to his father's property. Hamdi would remain with the landlord while Abdulahi relocated to a dirt floor storage room behind the house of the landlord's daughter. There, in the cramped windowless space, he hid and waited. Rats and cockroaches scampered across his legs as he tried to sleep on the hard ground at night. During the day, he lay still in blistering heat, flies crawling over his face. In this state of sweaty stupor, alone with his thoughts, Abdulahi grieved for his parents.

For two long months, Abdulahi stayed hidden in the storage room. The plan was for him to escape to South Africa, where a son of the landlord lived. A smuggler, arranged by the son, would provide transportation. In exchange for the help, Abdulahi ceded the inventory and operation of his family's shop to Farah. Hamdi—thought to be in less danger—would stay behind. They intended this separation to be temporary, but Abdulahi would never see his sister again.

# 5  *Foreigner*

South Africa to the U.S. Border

2005–2015

*Kwerekwere: Derogatory South African slang for foreigner.*

Abdulahi was running out of air. Wedged into the trunk of an older model black Mercedes-Benz sedan, he hoped the smuggler driving the car had enough incentive to deliver him alive to South Africa. Tensing his neck muscles to keep his head from hitting the floor with every bump in the road, Abdulahi banged the underside of the metal trunk door with the palm of his hand and shouted for the car to stop.

Grief had been Abdulahi's only companion during the two months he spent hiding in the storage room of the landlord's daughter. He was now on his way to start a new life, far from the Hawadle clan threat. The son of the landlord, Abshir, had arranged for the smuggler to transport Abdulahi. Under cover of darkness and dressed as a woman, he had escaped Beledwyne. This disguise had been the easiest part of the two-week, 3,200-mile trip.

Abshir lived outside Middelburg, South Africa, in the township— the area on the outskirts of the city where the White minority had forced the Black majority to live during apartheid. A midsize city located in an area known for coal mining and farming, Middelburg maintained a suburban feel, with broad, paved boulevards and large, shade-giving trees. But Middelburg was a city in decline. The global shift away from coal had sent the town into an economic slump with a double-digit unemployment rate, a growing population of homeless children, and high crime. Boarded-up storefronts lined the streets.

It was dusk when Abdulahi and the smuggler finally arrived at Abshir's home. A fence with a rolling gate surrounded the gold-toned, one-story cement house roofed with ceramic tiles. Bars protected the front door and windows. As the car pulled into the drive-way, Abshir stepped out to greet Abdulahi. Abshir then paid the smuggler. Abdulahi followed him inside to the kitchen table, where Abshir offered Abdulahi a simple supper of bariis ishkukaris, Somali spiced Basmati rice with goat meat—his first decent meal in months.

Abshir had lived in South Africa for over ten years, having settled there in the 1990s, after the civil war broke out in Somalia. While growing up in the same hometown in Somalia as Abdulahi, Abshir had been a student of Abdulahi's father. This relationship led Abshir to help Abdulahi escape from Somalia, but the smuggler was expensive, and Abshir expected repayment of the fee, the equivalent of $1,500. Abdulahi had come to an agreement with Abshir's father in Beledwyne, exchanging the contents of the family's shop for the landlord's assistance. But the shop goods had covered only the cost of sheltering Abdulahi in the storage room of Abshir's sister, not the long trip to South Africa. Abdulahi would have to work off his debt.

Abdulahi was safe, for the moment, but his life was not his own. His new home would be a clothing shop Abshir owned on the main street of the Middelburg township. By day, Abdulahi sold belts and socks on the street and helped in the back of the shop. By night, he provided security. He slept, ate, and spent the little free time he had in the stockroom. His indentured servitude would last one year. Abdulahi would remain in South Africa for a decade.

After repaying his debt to Abshir, Abdulahi took another year to establish himself in Middelburg. He applied to the South African authorities for asylum and was granted temporary refugee status. With the help of the Somali immigrant community, and endless hours of hard work, he opened his own store, selling long-distance calling cards, drinks, and other convenience-store items. He learned his trade through trial and error and was grateful for the advice of other local shopkeepers. He worked day and night, even sleeping in the shop.

Abdulahi met the woman who would become his first wife, Ifraah, on one of his trips to the sprawling Dragon City market in the city of Johannesburg to buy cheap stock for his shop. Ifraah was living with her sister and attending school in the Mayfair suburb of Johannesburg, near Fordsburg. She was just 19, yet she thought and acted like someone much older. She reveled in asking Abdulahi questions that he could not answer, like "What does God look like?" Science had the answers, not religion. Her irreverent intellect made Abdulahi smile. He liked her, a lot.

Ifraah's suburban community was nicknamed "Little Mogadishu" because of its large Somali population. Known for their skills as entrepreneurs, the Somali immigrants had built a local economy of restaurants, grocery shops, and gas stations. Like many of her neighbors, Ifraah had spent her early childhood in a Kenyan refugee camp because of the civil war. In South Africa, she was an asylum seeker. Like Abdulahi, she had applied for protection based on her fear of return to Somalia. Her mother still lived in the Kenyan refugee camp.

Ifraah's affection surprised Abdulahi at first. He had been struggling to turn a profit at his shop and could not promise Ifraah a comfortable life, or even a place to live. His asylum status was temporary and needed to be renewed every couple of years, which required paying a bribe to officials. But Ifraah pursued Abdulahi, encouraged by her older sister. After two years of friendship, Abdulahi gave her his heart. In late 2009, they were joined at her sister's house, in an unofficial, community marriage. A civil union was not possible. South Africa had strict practices regarding foreigners, especially asylum seekers who lacked permanent immigration status, like Abdulahi. The South African authorities would not issue them a marriage license.

In 2011, the couple welcomed a son, Muhammad. While Abdulahi continued to work long hours in the shop, he had learned how to make his business more profitable and was able to rent an apartment in the township of Middelburg for his family. Abdulahi and Ifraah spent their free time together, enjoying simple delights like pushing Muhammad in his stroller through local parks and eating Thai take-out in front of the TV. Abdulahi would later look back on this time with his wife and young son as the happiest of his adult life.

Then, during that same year, violence upended Abdulahi's life once again. He was at his shop, minding the cash register, as usual, when a neighboring shopkeeper burst in and warned him "Get out now!" There was an angry mob outside. Abdulahi needed no explanation. Hostility against foreigners had been brewing for years as South Africa struggled to overcome the legacy of apartheid. The official transition to democracy in 1994 did little to remedy the high wealth disparity that existed along racial lines. Over 20 percent of the country's people were unemployed. Immigrants like Abdulahi came from other parts of Africa, seeking refuge from political instability and food insecurity. They represented only a small fraction of the South African population. Yet they became scapegoats for the problems facing the young democracy.

Abdulahi scrambled out the back of his shop, just as the first attackers charged in, wielding large machetes called panga knives. They chanted "Kwerekwere!"—a derogatory term for foreigner meant to sound like gibberish, or like foreigners talking. Abdulahi ran. When he was a safe distance away, all he could do was call Ifraah to say, "Nothing is left. But I am alive." In the ten years that Abdulahi lived in South Africa, he and his shop would be targets of such xenophobic attacks three more times.

The worst occurred in late 2013. Two-year-old Muhammad was in day care. Ifraah was helping Abdulahi in the shop. Business had been brisk, and he had just expanded the store's inventory. Ifraah stood near the shop entrance, arranging shoes for sale on a wall rack. Abdulahi was behind the counter. The morning light streamed through the storefront windows. Outside, the wind was still. The door opened. Bells hanging on the top of the glass door jingled a welcome. When the door opened, Abdulahi could hear the rhythmic chant of the Toyi Toyi—a call and response song sung usually during protests, made popular during anti-apartheid demonstrations. Usually a joyous and life-affirming song, the Toyi Toyi was sometimes sung during xenophobic mob violence. Abdulahi looked toward the door. Three men barged into the shop, wielding sticks as weapons, with other men close behind. Before Abdulahi could react, the looters pushed Ifraah down and trampled over her. Two men rushed to grab Abdulahi, their main prey. He tried to maneuver out from behind the counter to help Ifraah, but the men slammed him onto the floor, beating and kicking him. As Ifraah and Abdulahi lay injured on the floor, the men turned their aggression to the shop, stripping the shelves and racks. More people from the growing mob outside streamed in. The shop, just minutes ago a place of quiet order, reverberated with mayhem as people took away everything they could carry. Abdulahi felt his right knee and shoulder throbbing. He endured the pain without moving, afraid to provoke another beating. After 30 long minutes, the store had been robbed of its entire contents, and the looters fled. The sounds of the Toyi Toyi became more and more distant as the mob moved further down the street.

Abdulahi crawled over to Ifraah. She had borne the brunt of the attack, hitting her head and eye on the edge of the counter as she was pushed down. Abdulahi brought her to the local hospital, where doctors tried to save her eye, without success. When they returned home, Ifraah stopped eating. In constant pain and unable to afford a scan of her head or additional medical care, she wept day and night. Her cries cut through Abdulahi deeper than any knife. Ifraah clung to their small son and wanted nothing but to return with him to her mother, in Kenya. Abdulahi could not deny what he knew would be Ifraah's last request. He hired a car to take her and Muhammad to the refugee camp in Kenya where Ifraah grew up and where her mother lived. Within months, Ifraah died of her injuries. Abdulahi would never see his son again.

His family and shop destroyed, Abdulahi left Middleburg's township for the city center, thinking it might be safer. He scouted an empty shop in a well-trafficked location, on a main road and near a taxi stand. With the skills to run a shop but no money, Abdulahi needed partners. He persuaded two men from the Somali community to go into business with him. They would provide the money. He would provide the expertise on running a business.

The local authorities did their best to shut the shop down. The police knew that Abdulahi's status as an asylum seeker meant that he could not obtain a business license. So the police threatened to close the shop, or get him deported, until Abdulahi paid them off. Abdulahi persisted, working 15-hour days. His hard work and business acumen transformed the small shop into a sizeable enterprise that sold everything from clothes and shoes to small electronics.

In 2014, another attack put an end to Abdulahi's small business career, forever. This time, the mob had fire tires—tires soaked in gasoline and lit up to "necklace" people to death. Abdulahi managed to escape injury, but the mob looted his shop and then burnt it to the ground. Abdulahi finally gave up on Middelburg and shopkeeping. He moved to Johannesburg and became a delivery driver.

Later in 2014, Abdulahi met his second wife, Fardowso. He had just purchased a Galaxy phone and had finished entering his contacts. Then he accidentally left the new phone at the restaurant of the hotel where he lived in Johannesburg. Fardowso, who worked at the restaurant, picked it up for safekeeping. When Abdulahi called the restaurant from a friend's phone, she said "Yes, I know who you are. I will hold it for you. By the way, my name is Fardowso."

A quick trip to retrieve the phone at Fardowso's apartment turned into an exchange of life stories. Fardowso, also Somali, had been abandoned by her husband. She lived alone, supporting herself by working at the restaurant. She, like Abdulahi, was Muslim. She wore a headscarf—usually in bold colors that set off her skin—draped around her head and shoulders.

Abdulahi was not sure he was ready to be with someone new. He was still grieving Ifraah, and he was not yet on sound financial footing in Johannesburg. Although Abdulahi was making a decent living, his income was still less than he had made as a shopkeeper. But he found himself wanting to spend time with Fardowso, and they started dating. For the first time since Ifraah's death, the weight of his losses began to lift.

Less than a year into their relationship, Fardowso got pregnant. Sex outside of marriage was not well-accepted in the Somali community, and it was taboo for a woman to have a child out of wedlock. Abdulahi and Fardowso were committed to one another and, in 2015, they were married at a Johannesburg mosque. Once again, Abdulahi could not obtain a civil license to marry from the South African authorities due to his status as an asylum seeker.

A few weeks later, Abdulahi was out working, making a delivery. He drove down a road on the outskirts of Johannesburg, a part of town that had been designated for Black people under apartheid. The legacy of oppression was visible wherever he looked. People lived in homes fashioned out of sheets of corrugated metal, crowded together, with no electricity or plumbing. Laundry hung out to dry on ropes strung between the makeshift shelters. Barefoot children kicked a soccer ball along the unpaved road. The stench of garbage and sewage hung in the air. The scene reminded Abdulahi of Somalia, although the poverty seemed worse, especially when juxtaposed with the White part of town just a mile away. In stark contrast to the neighborhood where he was driving, downtown Johannesburg boasted highways, skyscrapers, and a gleaming array of glass-front businesses.

Abdulahi's vehicle was full of packages yet to be dropped off. He stopped at a traffic light. The late-afternoon sun cast a blinding glare on the driver's side window. Waiting for the red light to turn green, Abdulahi saw out of the corner of his eye the dark outline of a man approaching. As the figure got closer, Abdulahi realized he had something in his hand. It was a gun, pointed straight at him.

Abdulahi knew not to resist. He opened the door and exited, his hands up. He took a few slow steps away from the car, carefully keeping his hands in view. He watched as the carjacker jumped into the vehicle and drove it away. Then Abdulahi walked to the nearest police station to get help and file a report. He waited a long time to be seen. When it was his turn, Abdulahi told the officer on duty what had happened. After the officer realized Abdulahi was a Somali asylum seeker, he said "Get out and don't come back. If you come back, we will deport you." Abdulahi didn't know which was worse: the carjacking or the refusal of the police to do their job because of who he was. It was at that moment that Abdulahi knew he would never be safe in South Africa.

That evening, Abdulahi took Fardowso's hand and explained what had happened. He waited for her to absorb his words and then implored, "Let's go to the United States." As Fardowso moved her other hand onto her belly, he added, "It's still early in the pregnancy. I'd like to raise our child in a country where we are accepted and safe from violence." Fardowso was unsure. It seemed too risky. And she would be leaving behind her closest family, her sister. But after much tearful conversation, the couple received Fardowso's sister's blessing to depart.

Ten years after Abdulahi had fled Somalia, his life was once again in the hands of smugglers. As low-income Somalis with no permanent status in South Africa, the doors to the visa office of the U.S. consulate in Johannesburg were closed to Abdulahi and Fardowso. They would have to find another way.

The plan was to fly to Brazil and then travel overland to the southern U.S. border, through Central America and Mexico. The agency arranging their trip said it wasn't a good idea for Abdulahi and Fardowso to take the same plane. "You go first. I will join you soon after," Abdulahi assured Fardowso.

On the day of her flight, Abdulahi waited outside in the airport parking lot while the smuggler they had hired walked Fardowso into the terminal building. After what seemed like too much time, the smuggler emerged. Abdulahi asked how things had gone. The smuggler had no answer; he was unable to confirm if Fardowso had boarded the plane. A day passed and there still was no word from Fardowso. Had she reached Brazil but been unable to call? Or had something gone wrong? The uncertainty tormented Abdulahi. Unless he was willing to sacrifice the money they had paid the smuggler, Abdulahi had no choice but to go forward with his own attempt as scheduled, in a couple of days.

Two agonizing days passed. In the end, Abdulahi decided to gamble that Fardowso had made it to Brazil. Following their original plan, he boarded his flight. The smugglers sent him to Ethiopia and then Togo, stops on the way to Brazil. He made it to São Paulo a full day later.

Fardowso resurfaced soon after. She was not in Brazil; she had never made it out of South Africa. The police had arrested her at the Johannesburg airport and held her for a few days. The smuggling agency could get her on another flight, this time through London, but would need more money. Abdulahi and Fardowso had the funds, but Fardowso despaired. "I can't do it again. It was terrible. I am staying here," she said.

Abdulahi was crushed by his wife's decision. Although he tried to persuade her, he would never see Fardowso again. He would never meet their son, Abdirahman Abdulahi Hassan.

After this blow, adjusting to Brazil was difficult. Abdulahi did not speak a word of Portuguese. Although he made it through the airport, the police stopped him on the street and took his fingerprints and picture, telling him to leave the country. Abdulahi made his way by bus to Peru, where he was also arrested for having no papers. He next passed through Ecuador, then Colombia.

Abdulahi was following a route well-worn by others seeking asylum in the United States. He would try to enter Panama by crossing over an infamously difficult mountain pass, the Darién Gap, on the border between Colombia and Panama. In 2021, over 100,000 people risked their lives on the trail. This remote jungle area is so difficult to traverse that it is the single break along the Pan-American Highway, which stretches from the southern tip of Argentina to Prudhoe Bay, Alaska. The road north ends in the coastal town of Turbo, Colombia, and does not pick up again until Yaviza, Panama, on the other side of the Darién mountains. In Yaviza, a sign in Spanish reads, "Welcome to Yaviza, 12,580 kilometers to the highway's end, in Alaska."

Abdulahi traveled the Pan-American highway to Turbo and then boarded a boat to cross the Gulf of Urabá to where the Darién Gap trail begins. Two dozen passengers, mainly asylum seekers headed for the United States from Africa, overloaded the 25-foot open boat. As the outboard motor labored, Abdulahi checked his backpack and felt his pocket for his cellphone.

The boat trip lasted two hours. Wind in the open bay generated six-foot swells. As the boat lurched up and down, the passengers, many of whom could not swim, held on as tightly as they could to quell their terror. Some distance from the opposite shore, the swells subsided to

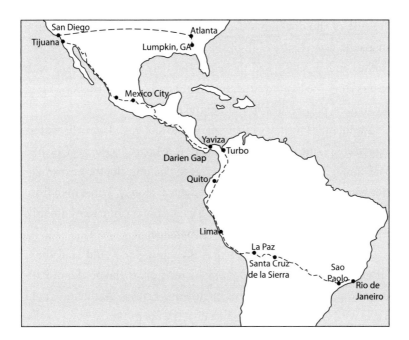

Abdulahi's route to seek asylum in the United States. Courtesy of Thomas W. Sharpless.

choppy water. Yet the captain cut the engine. He had spied green uniformed officers massed at the landing. Rather than get caught transporting migrants, the captain ordered everyone off the boat, trying to force them into the water. The two men forming his crew shouted at the passengers in Spanish, pointing overboard and tossing people's belongings into the water. Abdulahi and the other passengers looked at each other in panic. The crew had begun shoving people overboard, ignoring all pleas. Abdulahi saw he had no choice. He clutched his backpack and jumped, swimming for his life, and thankful for his childhood efforts at swimming in the Shabelle River.

Abdulahi swam for 15 minutes. He made it to land, without his backpack, which he lost in the water. He reached the beach well to the side of the docking area, so as not to attract attention. In the chaos, he wasn't sure if all of the passengers made it to shore. His clothes and shoes soaked through, Abdulahi sat on the beach with others from the boat to catch his breath and dry out. He hoped that the hardest part of the trip was behind him.

Abdulahi's journey to Panama would not get easier. His waterlogged cellphone no longer worked. Before boarding the boat, he had paid smugglers to take him all the way to Panama. But the next smuggler who met him on land demanded more money. Three men from Eritrea, who had swum alongside him to shore, came to Abdulahi's rescue, pooling money to pay for his passage.

The deal they struck was that the smuggler would lead them through the last stretch of Colombian territory to the border of Panama. In addition to the three men from Eritrea, Abdulahi would travel with eight Ghanaians and a dozen Cubans.

The group set off and walked together for an hour. At that point, the smuggler stopped short, pointing ahead. "Follow this river to Panama. It is eight hours to walk." With that, he turned around and left Abdulahi and the others standing in thick mud, surrounded by the endless green of the jungle.

The route turned out not to be an eight-hour walk, but an eight-*day* trek through the treacherous rainforest that covered a vast mountainous area. It rained constantly in the thick jungle—one of the wettest places in the world. Abdulahi and his companions feared the animals lurking under impenetrable vegetation, including venomous snakes and scorpions. The group was completely exposed when resting at night, with barely any food. The racket of frogs kept them awake in the dark. They dreaded being attacked or robbed by drug traffickers who used the same, trash-strewn trail. Abdulahi and the others would eventually make their way through 60 miles of nearly impassable mountainous jungle to traverse the Darién Gap. For many desperate migrants, this is the most dangerous section of their journey to the U.S.–Mexico border. Some perish in the attempt. Abdulahi trudged past two bodies, fallen beside the path.

On the fourth morning of the trip, Abdulahi and his companions reached a steep part of the trail. Abdulahi walked in the middle of their single file group, ignoring the crippling pangs of hunger and the open sores on his feet. Ankle-deep mud made each step a struggle. The group reached a four-foot wall of mud across the trail and stopped. There was no way to walk around it. The only way forward was up and over the barrier. Abdulahi helped the person ahead of him with a leg up and then accepted a hand. Over the next hours, they scrambled up dozens of these giant steps. A few people behind Abdulahi, a man from Ghana was gasping and cursing over the ascents. But by the time the sun cast long shadows over the trail, he fell silent. When the group stopped for the night, he was not with them. Abdulahi never saw him again.

After eight days, the remaining group, on the brink of starvation, arrived at an encampment of thatched huts—a Panamanian border-control base. Machine-gun-toting men in camouflage uniforms offered neither food nor shelter. Sick with a fever and chills, Abdulahi encountered a small group of Somali men and women nearby. They helped him, paying the $40 for his river-boat crossing to the next Panamanian base. It was only at a third border-control base that Abdulahi found any shelter and food, though no medical care. Panamanian border officials took Abdulahi's fingerprints and, using biometric screening equipment supplied by the United States, scanned his eyes, telling him he had 15 days to leave Panama. Abdulahi couldn't believe he was still alive. He was more than happy to keep moving to Yaviza, Panama City, and then Costa Rica.

With fresh funds wired to him by Fardowso, Abdulahi next traveled by train, bus, and car through Central America and Mexico. It took him four more weeks before he ended up at the U.S. border near Tijuana, where he told U.S. immigration officials his story.

Abdulahi had traveled for three months, through nine countries, to seek safe refuge in the United States. He had been left to drown, then barely survived the Darién Gap. Yet what awaited Abdulahi in the United States was not safety. When he declared his intention to apply for asylum, ICE detained him. Shackled at his wrists, waist, and ankles, Abdulahi was shipped to a private prison owned by Corrections Corporation of America: the Stewart Detention Center in Lumpkin, Georgia, which is the nation's largest immigration detention facility, located hours from the nearest city. Abdulahi would spend the next two years locked up. He would lose his asylum case in front of an immigration judge known for denying nearly every single asylum case that came before her, and ultimately be loaded onto the ICE Air Flight N225AX for deportation to Somalia on December 7, 2017.

# 6  *The Struggle*

Dakar, Senegal

DECEMBER 8, 2017

*ICE Special Response Team (SRT): An elite group of immigration law enforcement officers trained at the Fort Benning military base in Georgia to use force and tactical gear against noncitizens.*

Flight N225AX was going nowhere. Sa'id could hardly believe what the man shuffling down the aisle had said: They were not waiting for a part from the United States; the plane was not being fixed; they were stuck on the tarmac in Senegal. Sa'id turned to Nadim, seated next to him in the back of the plane, "They lied to us." The plane was not broken. Something else was going on—something ICE was keeping secret.

With ICE's lie exposed, the sense of betrayal rushed through the airplane cabin like a flash flood on a dry stream bed. Shouts of disbelief and anger erupted in English and Somali. Many got to their feet. "We want answers," Sa'id implored of the closest officer, the spoken word his only resistance. "Sit the fuck back down," responded the officer, a member of the ICE Special Response Team. He would provide no answers. More men stood up, demanding to speak with someone from the Somali Embassy or the United Nations. More SRT officers shoved them back into their seats, into submission, a grim game of human Whack-A-Mole.

An SRT officer opened up a luggage carrier over the seat, grabbed some disposable gloves and put them on. They were red, as if the officer was expecting his hands to get bloody and didn't want it to show.

Abdulahi, seated nearer the front, heard shouts at the back of the plane. He raised himself up a few inches and craned his neck to try and look over the back of his seat but couldn't see what was happening. When word reached him about ICE's lie, he understood what the shouts were about. Having been in detention for so long, Abdulahi was no longer surprised by the actions of U.S. immigration officers. Although some had displayed decency, others reminded him of the police officers he had met in South Africa who had treated him as an unwanted foreigner and failed to protect him.

Sa'id muttered to Nadim, "We need to get out. Head for the back door." Nadim occupied the aisle seat, so he moved first. When he saw an opening in the tangle of shackled men and officers, he rose and walked down the aisle toward the rear as fast as his ankle chains allowed. Sa'id tried to follow, but Nadim's movement had attracted the officers' attention. The one closest to Sa'id intercepted him, stepping on his ankle chains, then slamming him hard. As Sa'id fell, his cuffed right hand—the one with the damaged pinky—slammed into an armrest. The pain paralyzed his body. Sa'id wondered if he would need surgery on his hand. Regaining control, Sa'id struggled upright and tried again to move toward the plane's rear door. All around him, men were rising from their seats, crowding, pushing, desperate to get off the plane, to be free. Flailing hands and elbows, faces full of fear and anger, filled the cabin. In response, SRT officers massed at the back of the plane. They kicked and shoved the men, stepping on their ankle chains to send them crashing down. "Sit your asses down, motherfuckers!" they barked. "We have one job and that's to get rid of you by all means!"

The violence washed around Sa'id. To his left, an officer stood on a seat, kicking men in the aisles in the chest. To his right, another officer grabbed the torso and legs of a small Somali man, turned him upside down, and threw him to the floor. More officers dragged people down the aisle. The SRT officers, some masked, knew how to use force to overwhelm the protesting people. They had done it many times before. Don't leave a mark. Avoid drawing blood. Broken noses are messy.

The masked overseers were faceless and nameless, having removed the Velcro name tags on their uniforms. They could do anything to their prisoners, and no one would ever know.

Sa'id watched as the dozens of spent men mustered their last strength to fight back, to recapture their humanity and break free. He could hardly believe what was happening around him—on a flight arranged and funded by the U.S. government. He had seen chaos and raw emotion like this before, during Somalia's civil war. The United States was supposed to be different.

Rows away, an SRT officer ordered Abdulahi, his friend Ibrahim, and several men and women near them to move closer to the front of the plane, where the non-SRT officers and nurses were sitting. Abdulahi and Ibrahim complied. Some of the others did not, preferring to remain near the protestors. The officer had drawn a line: good Africans in front; bad ones in back. Hearing louder shouts behind them, Abdulahi and Ibrahim swapped guarded looks. It was not hard to imagine what was happening, even as an officer warned two Somali women seated in front of them, "Don't look back."

The dividing line was not lost on Abdulahi. Resisting the officers while in bondage was futile. He knew the men in back realized this. Yet they struggled anyway. Abdulahi faced an impossible choice. Join the resistance, as a show of solidarity, and risk injury. Or acquiesce and move to the front, avoiding harm. Abdulahi knew the stakes. He and his first wife Ifraah had suffered ruthless violence in South Africa. He had survived. She had not.

"He's going for a gun," shouted a Somali man in the back of the plane, near Sa'id, pointing at an officer. Sa'id didn't see a gun, but it was the last straw for him. He collapsed into the nearest seat, bruised and battered, his pants torn. He examined his right hand. It was bad. Very bad. He couldn't move his pinky finger. Some men had blood on their shirts; at least one man was in a straitjacket; others were cradling bruised or injured limbs. The officers' orders and expletives mixed with the shackled men's cries of pain and anger. The resistance was over. Sa'id thought the Somalis in the front of the plane should have joined the struggle. With their help, they all might have gotten to the back door. After all, they were in this together.

An officer approached Sa'id, pointing. "You, come with me." It was Sa'id's turn to be summoned to the front of the plane. Sa'id walked past dozens of rows filled with men in states of desperate disarray—on the floor struggling to stand up, leaning on seats trying to catch their breath, collapsed in seats. He walked past the section where Abdulahi and the other, nonresisting men and the two women, sat. No one looked at Sa'id as he moved past. In the first-class section, the ICE supervisor—a tall White man with salt and pepper hair—stood waiting. Sa'id slowed to a halt, meeting eyes that looked him up and down. Sa'id had been identified as a leader. With the SRT officers there to back him up, the ICE supervisor could afford to be calm. Sa'id listened to the rush of the air from the plane's air conditioning system, waiting for the supervisor to speak.

"Here's the problem," the supervisor said. "We can now take off, but we have missed the window to land in Djibuti, where another plane was supposed to take you to Mogadishu. We can wait for the window to reopen. Or we can return to the U.S."

After a brief pause, Sa'id squinted, looked right at the supervisor, and stated the obvious. "You can't keep us caged up like this. Let us go, or at least take us back to the United States. Give us what you can to make us more comfortable." He glanced around him. "Look, you have sodas, Snickers, and blueberry muffins."

The ICE supervisor nodded, although he took no interest in Sa'id's opinion. He had already decided to take the airplane back to the United States. What he wanted was for Sa'id to exert his influence to control the other men.

Sa'id had no idea whether he would be allowed to stay in the United States if the plane returned there. But he would take his chances. Perhaps his lawyer could find a way to prevent ICE from deporting him again. He would take things one day at a time, as he had for so many years in the refugee camps, time after time walking with his mother to the refugee office to check for their names on the list. If there was one thing Sa'id knew, it was how to do time.

The ICE supervisor led Sa'id to the front door of the plane, to the phone connected to the intercom. He handed Sa'id the handset and asked him to tell the others what was happening and to remain calm. In Somali and English, Sa'id repeated what the supervisor had explained. He then said, "We fought, and we lost. Let's go back home," and promised sodas and snacks. As Sa'id walked back down the aisle, taking care with each step and turning his head left and right to meet the eyes of the others, some men held up their shackles and shook them, as in victory. Cheers rose and filled the cabin. But not from everyone. Some had endured years in U.S. detention in failed bids for asylum. They understood that a return to the United States would mean more time locked up and most likely another deportation flight.

Sa'id returned to his seat, injured and weary but full of hope. He turned to Nadim, who greeted him with a smile. "It's a miracle."

# 7  *Glades County Jail*

Moore Haven, Florida

DECEMBER 9, 2017

*Glades Correctional Development Corporation was formed in 2002 by leaders in Glades County, Florida, to build a $33-million medium security jail to detain people for ICE.*

The ICE bus barreled down Florida's old two-lane highway, Route 27, headed north, away from Miami. Sa'id rested his forehead against the tinted window. He was shackled. Light from a half moon illuminated limitless fields of sugar cane crossed by canals. Smoke rose over the flat land from the burning of cane leaves before harvest of the stalks. It was before dawn on Saturday, December 9, 2017. Flight N225AX had returned to the United States the night before, landing at 9:25 p,m. at the Miami airport, 39 hours after its original departure from Louisiana. Sa'id hadn't slept since the night of Wednesday, December 5. He wondered where ICE was taking him now.

At the Miami airport, a new team of SRT officers with riot gear and automatic weapons had surrounded the aircraft while the 92 Somali men and women, still shackled, shuffled off the plane. They were hustled into an ICE bus and shuttled to Krome Service Processing Center, a 50-year-old federal detention center on the outskirts of the city. Some of the men would stay at Krome. But Sa'id, together with about 50 other men and the two women, had been jammed into holding cells for hours and given a peanut butter and jelly sandwich. In the middle of the night, officers loaded them onto another bus to Glades County Detention Center, a county jail in the central Florida town of Moore Haven.

Although only two and a half hours north of Miami, Moore Haven is a world away. The town boasts eight churches but no mosque or synagogue. One Mexican restaurant is the only visible evidence of the area's immigrant community. Glades County is home to 12,884 people—the fourth least-populated county in Florida. Only 1,566 people live in the town of Moore Haven itself. Over half of them are incarcerated, either at Glades County Jail or at the private prison across the street, owned and operated by GEO Group.

Moore Haven sits on the bank of Lake Okeechobee, the eighth largest natural lake in the United States. Zora Neale Hurston wrote how, in 1928, the "monstropolous beast" broke through the log dike meant to contain it and drowned 1,825 people, including many who worked cutting sugar cane. Today, a 40-foot dike of earth and cement has tamed the beast and largely obscures it from view. A network of government canals controls the water from the lake. These interventions have restricted the water's natural flow out of the lake and drained the surrounding wetlands to create dry land for farming and development. The area used to be part of a vast "river of grass" that spanned 100 miles from the lake to Florida's west coast.

Clewiston, one town south of Moore Haven, is home to the U.S. Sugar Company. Its headquarters—a well-kept two-story building of white pillars and red bricks—reflect Big Sugar's status as a $10-billion-a-year, government-subsidized industry. But Florida's sugar money does not trickle down to the people of Moore Haven. For decades, sugar companies had employed thousands of workers, including many immigrants, to select and cut cane by hand. Cutting by hand is backbreaking work, and growers drew criticism for treating cane cutters "like slaves." Rather than raise wages and improve labor conditions, the companies discharged the workers and switched to machines for cane cutting and burning. Today, over 20 percent of Moore Haven's residents live below the poverty line.

With its economy in decline, Glades County was on the hunt for jobs and revenue. One source was traffic tickets. County police officers positioned themselves at the south edge of Moore Haven, near the Mexican restaurant, where an overpass dumps traffic going 65 miles an hour into a 35 mile-per-hour zone. In 2002, Glades County leadership had another idea: Build a new jail to hold people for ICE. Counties across the nation were raking in federal money and creating local correctional jobs by incarcerating immigrants. Glades County wanted in on the action.

Four years later, county commissioners and other Glades County leaders formed Glades Correctional Development Corporation, or GCDC, for the sole purpose of building the new jail. Revenue bonds to fund the facility were issued on March 14, 2006, and, by 2007, GCDC had completed construction. At 500 beds, the jail was many times over the size needed to meet the criminal custody needs of the sparsely populated Glades County. The jail entered a contract with ICE to hold people for $80 a day per person, a rate that was raised to $90 in 2017. As the Internal Revenue Service would later observe in a letter, GCDC's contract with the federal government was "an opportunity to offer beds for rental" to immigration, "producing economic benefits to the County." Immigration "inmates represent[ed] over 85% of all inmates in the facility."

But the new Glades County Detention Center did not generate the levels of revenue the commissioners had envisioned. The federal government was not sending enough people to Glades for the county to turn a profit. Years before Sa'id and the other Somali men and women arrived at Glades, county commission minutes reflected

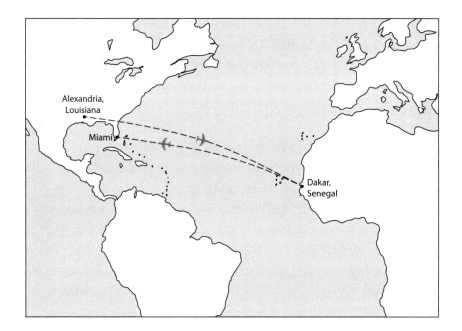

The route of ICE Air Flight N225AX. Courtesy of Thomas W. Sharpless.

money concerns. Then, in early 2017, during the Trump Administration, the financial picture started to improve.

The county commission's February 14, 2017, meeting started with a prayer and the pledge of allegiance. Addressing the all-White commission, Commissioner John Ahern, the owner of the main gas station in town, reported that the jail was able to make timely payment on its bills for the first time in two years. The jail "was headed in the right direction," he said. He even hinted at expansion of the contract with ICE to hold more women at the county's old jail—the facility that Glades County Detention Center had abandoned in 2006.

By the time Sa'id and the other Somali men and women reached Glades, the jail was holding 400 men and women for ICE, close to the highest number in five years. The addition of the Somalis would help Glades reach its most profitable quarter in years. On February 26, 2018, two months after ICE brought Sa'id to Glades, the county commission minutes reported that there were "504 inmates being housed at the facility," and GCDC had just experienced "one of its best fiscal quarters since 2012."

The ICE bus pulled into the secure area of Glades through a gate in a 12-foot fence topped with coils of barbed wire. Sa'id and the other men and women filed off the bus and into a single-story, white concrete block processing unit. With a few clicks of a universal cuff key, Sa'id's wrists, waist, and ankles were at last released. He was unbound but still confined.

Usual protocol was for all new arrivals to go through an intake procedure, where computer checks were run, clothing was issued, and a medical screening was performed. But it had been two days since Flight N225AX had taken off from Louisiana. Glades staff made a rare decision favoring the men and women's intense need for sleep. The processing would wait. Correctional officers escorted Sa'id and the others down windowless hallways, through heavy security doors, and into lit living pods.

Sa'id took in his new surroundings. The pod resembled others he had been in: A large living area with a high ceiling and rows of tables, flanked by two stories of three-walled, six-person cubicles or cells. A stairway with a metal handrail led to the upper-floor cells. The walls were off-white cinder block, the floor gray cement. Everything—the floor, walls, telephones, chairs, and tables—looked older than it was, a product of neglect. Each of the two levels had a bathroom that was entirely open to the pod's main room. Anyone showering or using the toilet was on full display to the other detained people and officers. A surveillance post in the main area allowed officers to simultaneously monitor the seating area, the cells on both levels, and the bathrooms. All activities, including sleeping, eating, and watching television, would occur in this pod. The only time any detained person would leave was for the one daily hour of outdoor recreation or a medical appointment, or to use the closet-sized law library.

Still dressed in his torn khaki pants and white polo shirt, Sa'id made his way to the far side of the two-story living unit, where an officer assigned him to one of the small cells ringing the common area on the first floor. He crawled into a bottom bunk and lay down, his exhaustion an analgesic for his damaged right hand. As Sa'id collapsed onto the bed, he felt knobby metal springs through the thin mattress. It seemed like paradise.

# 8   *Krome Service Processing Center*

Miami, Florida

DECEMBER 15, 2017

*A person in immigration court has "the privilege of being represented, at no expense to the Government."*

IMMIGRATION AND NATIONALITY ACT

On December 15, 2017, six days after ICE Air Flight N225AX flew back from Senegal and landed in Miami, Abdulahi was detained at Krome, 100 miles away from Glades. He sat on one of four blue plastic stools affixed to a round table in one of the living units. His friend, Ibrahim, and a handful of other men from the flight, were locked up with him. Three of the men, including Ibrahim, joined Abdulahi at the table and discussed their predicament. Was ICE going to put them on another plane in just a few days?

Abdulahi wore a blue short-sleeve uniform that designated him as a low security threat. Long rows of metal bunk beds lined up dormitory style a few feet away from him. A 12-foot ceiling with fluorescent lights topped the white concrete block walls of the cavernous room. A uniformed correctional officer watched from a raised platform with a counter that served as a security post. A TV hung on the wall in front of large, cream-colored plastic chairs that looked like lounge chairs but were hard as rocks. Outside, immigration officers practiced shooting their guns at a target range. With each shot, Abdulahi flinched.

Located at the edge of the Everglades, on the outskirts of Miami, Krome is one of the country's oldest detention centers. The federal government built the facility in 1965, three years after the Cuban missile crisis, as a Cold War–era military defense base. Concrete missile pads, now overgrown with weeds, still dot the grounds. As the Cold War waned, the base fell into disuse until some 125,000 Cuban men, women, and children arrived on Miami's shores during the Mariel boatlift in 1980. The federal government converted Krome into a temporary immigration processing center. Over the next decade, the United States constructed hangar-like dormitories and filled them with immigrants, primarily asylum seekers from Haiti fleeing the dictatorship of Jean-Claude "Baby Doc" Duvalier. Immigration judges started hearing deportation cases in trailers fashioned into courtrooms.

One of these judges, Neale Strong Foster, was the country's longest serving federal employee before his death in 2006. He worked for the federal government for 59 years—20 of those years at Krome, where he ordered the deportation of almost every person appearing before him. From 2000 to 2005, he denied 94.6 percent of the asylum cases before him, the third highest denial rate in the country at the time. By contrast, the immigration judge with the third lowest denial rate at that time denied only 17.3 percent of asylum cases. A letter contained in a 1989 Senate report described how Judge Foster deported eight people from Haiti in ten minutes after failing to advise them of their right to apply for asylum. In his later years, he was known to fall asleep while on the bench. Judge Foster continued hearing cases at Krome until his death at age 81.

During the years Judge Foster presided at Krome, the detention center had developed a national reputation as a place of abuse, corruption, and exploitation. In 1990, the FBI started an investigation into criminal misconduct of correctional officers. A year later, two human rights groups documented physical and sexual abuse, improper use of solitary confinement, and overcrowding. These reports had no effect, and Krome became so overcrowded that people had to be held in tents. The chief of the Public Health Service Clinic at the center warned in 1995 that the extreme overcrowding would lead to "serious health consequences." A government accountability team admonished Krome officials for moving detained people to other facilities in advance of an inspection in an attempt to hide the continued overcrowding from inspectors.

In 2000, the federal government opened a series of investigations into sexual assault and corruption allegations. Women had reported being pressured to have sex with jail authorities in exchange for release. A correctional officer was indicted for raping a woman who had applied for asylum. Another officer was convicted of having sex with a detained woman in an attorney visitation booth used by the local nonprofit organization Florida Immigrant Advocacy Center. One Krome employee pled guilty to accepting $1,000 in exchange for letting a detained person use a cellphone. Detained people described an unruly party atmosphere in which drugs flowed freely. In 2000, as a response to the scandals, immigration authorities moved all women out of Krome to a higher security, harsher, county jail in Miami. After Glades was built in 2006, ICE transported the women there.

By the time Abdulahi arrived at Krome in late 2017, ICE had started to clean up its act. The detention center was now regarded as one of better places to be locked up, especially as compared to Glades. Relatively speaking, Abdulahi was lucky.

Abdulahi didn't realize he was fortunate. Nor did he know that local lawyers were mobilizing to try to help him and the others on Flight N225AX. Word of the abusive imprisonment on the plane had spread through the

Somali community in Minnesota, home to a large part of the U.S. Somali diaspora and many people on the flight. On Wednesday, December 13, 2017, *Newsweek* reporter Carlos Ballesteros interviewed Rahim Mohamed, a Somali man from the flight who was detained at Glades. The 32-year-old truck driver and father of two had lived in the United States as a lawful permanent resident since 2002. Rahim did not mince his words when he explained over the jail phone: "We were treated like slaves. We were shackled for nearly two days. We weren't allowed to use the bathroom or get out of the plane. I was not given the medication I need. I peed into a bottle, and then I peed on myself. It was a horrible thing, man. I thought my life was pretty much over."

After speaking with Rahim, Carlos Ballesteros contacted ICE by email at 1:47 p.m. that same day. Nine minutes later, a spokesperson responded with a seven-sentence statement. ICE declared that nothing out of the ordinary had occurred during the two-day flight. There was no mention of any delay on the tarmac in Senegal due to a part being flown from the United States. Rather, the statement maintained that the grounding resulted from the relief aircraft crew in Senegal not getting sufficient rest because of a problem with their hotel. "Lavatories were functional and serviced the entire duration of the trip. The allegations of ICE mistreatment onboard the Somali flight are categorically false. No one was injured during the flight, and there were no incidents or altercations that would have caused any injuries on the flight." In other words, anyone who spoke of abuse and neglect on Flight N225AX was a liar.

ICE had chosen the path of blanket denial.

The next day, a law school professor in Minneapolis, who had a client on the flight, called a law school professor in Miami and told her that a deportation flight to Somalia had turned around and landed in Miami. People had been shackled for two days and abused. *Newsweek* had run a story. Could Miami lawyers do something to help?

As Abdulahi sat in detention talking to Ibrahim and the other men on Friday, December 15, 2017, a team of lawyers had already arrived at Krome and were arranging to speak with him and others from the flight. A correctional officer entered the unit and called out "Somalia" with the last three digits of Abdulahi's alien number, or A-number, the eight-digit identifier assigned to him by ICE. In Somalia, boys from the Hawadle clan called him the name of his clan, Shiqaal, instead of his name. Here in the United States, Abdulahi was called by a number and his country. Abdulahi looked up from his conversation. The officer announced, "legal visit."

Abdulahi was buoyed but confused. A lawyer? He had not had an attorney since his failed bid for asylum in the Georgia detention center a year earlier. Who could be visiting?

Abdulahi accepted the officer's escort out of the pod. Unlike Glades, where detained people spent almost all their time inside, Krome's buildings were separated by large expanses of grass. Detainees breathed fresh air when officers took them to the cafeteria for meals or the medical unit. As Abdulahi walked in front of the correctional officer in the humid morning air, his knee—the one injured in the attack in South Africa—twinged with pain. Abdulahi's ankles and wrists were also still hurting from the two days of tight metal shackles. Even as his body started to heal, Abdulahi struggled with the lingering mental effects of the long and growing list of traumas he had endured. He had been kidnapped and forced to listen to his sister's screams while she was raped in Somalia; his parents were murdered when he was 18; his first wife, Ifraah, had been killed by xenophobic mob violence in South Africa, and their child was in Kenya; his second wife, Fardowso, remained in South Africa and had given birth to their child; he had barely survived the deadly trek through the Darién Gap; and most recently, he had been shackled and immobilized for almost two days on Flight N225AX. Any one of these events alone would have threatened his mental health but together they were more than anyone could be expected to bear.

In a large holding cell outside the legal visitation booths, Abdulahi sat down on a bench, near other Somali men waiting for lawyers. Rumors ran amok: Lawyers were interested in what had happened to them on the flight and wanted to help. But what did that mean? Were they going to try and stop the next plane?

After an hour of waiting, Abdulahi heard an officer call out the last three digits of his A-number again. He stood up and followed the officer down a short, narrow corridor, through a windowed door, and into a small room with glass on three sides, framed by blue-painted metal, with just enough space for a table and two plastic chairs. A red button on the wall was for attorneys to set off a buzzer if they wanted to contact a correctional officer. Another door—for the attorneys—led to a second hallway where Abdulahi could see similar rooms.

"Hi, have a seat. Do you speak English?" The lawyer from the hastily assembled legal team sat at the table and extended a smile and a hand. She had a ballpoint pen, a notepad, and a blank form of some kind. Abdulahi told her that he did speak some English and asked how she got his name. He just couldn't think of who would have contacted lawyers on his behalf. The attorney explained that the Somali Embassy had provided a list of everyone on the plane. "We're trying to talk to as many people as we can today and this weekend," she said.

The lawyer then launched into questions, seemingly as listed on the form: "Do you have family in the United States? An immigration lawyer? What happened on the flight?" The questions kept coming. The purpose was not clear. "Can you help me?" Abdulahi asked when there was a slight pause. He was still afraid of returning to Somalia, but he was wary of spending any more time locked up with no end in sight. Before the botched deportation flight, he had already lost almost two years of his life.

The attorney's answer was noncommittal. She wasn't sure what could be done. She would go over notes from their interview with other attorneys on the team and discuss possible next steps, if any. "Do you want to try and stay in the United States?" she asked.

Abdulahi hesitated, then responded, "If you will help, yes." It seemed futile to try and stay and fight without a lawyer, but if he had one, maybe there was reason for optimism. Abdulahi remembered the way some men had reacted when the announcement came that the plane was returning to the United States, so he knew he wasn't speaking for everyone. Some people wanted to avoid further ICE detention at all costs.

Abdulahi had good reason to fight his deportation to Somalia, even if it meant more time in detention. His wife Fardowso was in South Africa, and he had no family alive in Somalia. He had received word that his sister Hamdi had also managed to flee their home country after their parents were killed. Abdulahi didn't know where she was. Most importantly, the men who had murdered his parents still had a motive to come after him because he had a claim to the title of his parents' house. Abdulahi told the lawyer what happened to him in Somalia and South Africa. The lawyer listened, acknowledging his story with a gentle nod. She would see what could be done. But, again, she made no promises.

Later that evening, back in the living unit, Abdulahi, Ibrahim, and their companions swapped accounts of their legal visits. Ibrahim had also spoken to a lawyer. He had asked her whether she was going to try and stop the plane. He was desperate to return to his wife and children in Atlanta. When the lawyer told him she was not sure, he stressed that she would have to act fast if she wanted to help. News had spread through Krome that ICE was going to make a second attempt to deport the 92 Somalis in a few days. Flight N225AX had left Louisiana early in the morning of December 7, returning to the United States and landing in Miami in the evening of the 8th. The

*Newsweek* story had broken on Thursday, December 14, 2017. ICE's second flight was rumored to be scheduled for December 19 or 20. It was already Friday, December 15. If the lawyers were going to do something, they had to act fast.

The next day, a Saturday, Ibrahim was called for a second legal visit. When he returned, Abdulahi and other Somali men crowded around him, eager for news. Ibrahim announced that the attorneys would file a lawsuit to stop the next plane and, if successful, would help them fight their deportations. Ibrahim had agreed to be part of the lawsuit and had signed documents, including a sworn declaration about what had happened on Flight N225AX. The lawsuit would be filed on behalf of everyone who had been on the plane. As Ibrahim recounted his conversation with the lawyer, Abdulahi closed his eyes to absorb the sweet sensation of hope.

As Abdulahi had predicted, not everyone wanted to stay and fight. Some wanted no further delay to their deportation. Stopping the flight would mean more time in ICE custody. Unless some legal tactic could gain their release and permission to remain in the United States, halting the plane seemed just delaying the inevitable. Others wanted to try and stay, at least if they had a lawyer to help them with their case. Most had had no lawyer, or no competent lawyer, the first time they appeared before an immigration judge. Like Abdulahi, many of the men would take any chance they could to stay in the United States.

Over a dozen volunteer lawyers from nonprofit and private law offices had responded to the Minnesota and Miami law professors' call for help. Over the weekend, some of these attorneys rushed to speak with over 30 Somali women and men, at both Krome and Glades. There was not enough time to poll everyone who had been on the flight. The attorneys were not even sure a majority of the group of 92 approved of the lawsuit. But they knew that at least 30, including Abdulahi and Ibrahim, were determined to stay and fight. That seemed like enough.

*PART II*

PART II.

# 9  *Stay of Deportation*

Miami, Florida

DECEMBER 19, 2018

*Injunction: Court order preventing the carrying out of an action.*

BLACK'S LAW DICTIONARY

Sa'id rolled over in his bunk, hoping to rest a bit longer. It was 5 a.m., the standard wake-up time at Glades. The schedule skewed early, as if the jail administrators wanted to make sure detained people took advantage of daylight hours, even though there was nothing to do except watch television. Meals were also much earlier than was customary, with breakfast at 5:30 or 6 a.m., lunch at 10:30 or 11 a.m., and dinner around 5 p.m.

Sa'id had been at Glades just over a week, long enough to learn the daily routine plus the major dos and don'ts. Do keep to oneself. Avoid conflict and keep one's mouth shut. Don't raise concerns, ask for things, or talk to officers more than absolutely necessary. Even knowing these rules, Sa'id found it hard to swallow his dignity when confronted with some officers' behavior. Some called the detained men "monkeys," "boys," or "niggers." The steady stream of verbal abuse took its toll. For some of the men, the treatment they endured at Glades caused them to act less like themselves. Sa'id watched men's self-esteem, and sometimes their self-control, wither away.

As breakfast was being served, Sa'id pulled himself out of bed, slipped into his jail-issued flip-flops, and headed to the bathroom. He wore an ID bracelet and a white T-shirt under a short-sleeved uniform in red, the color that marked him as having a serious criminal record. All of the space was communal, with no provision for privacy. Often at least one of the toilets was not working, and the bathroom usually reeked of urine and feces. As in most immigration jails, the detained people were responsible for the cleaning, although keeping Glades truly clean was difficult. The men were not allowed to use bleach.

Sa'id lined up for a breakfast tray. He kept his expectations low. Meals at Glades were not only of marginal nutritional quality but were doled out in such small portions that they did not even supply daily caloric requirements. This morning's meal was two spoonfuls of scrambled eggs made from powder, a piece of moldy white bread, and a juice cup. Sa'id needed to eat so he wouldn't lose too much weight. The gnaw of hunger in his belly sent him back to the Kenyan refugee camps, where there was so little food that he continually felt hungry. Sa'id would do whatever he could to stave off that awful sensation.

He sat with several other Somali men from the flight and poked at his eggs. He chewed mechanically, knowing that lunch—probably a bologna sandwich—would not be any better. He hoped that Janene had been able to add money into his commissary account so he could purchase some ramen noodles. Beside him, the other men talked, raising their voices to make themselves heard over the background noise in the pod. There was no escaping the constant clamor, amplified by the cavernous room's concrete walls: men talking and the blare of the TV, punctuated by announcements, buzzes, and alarms. The men were allowed out of this cacophony once on weekdays, for one hour of recreation. Recreation took place outside, in a barren dirt area enclosed by more concrete walls. But at least Sa'id could see the sky. In the week since Flight N225AX had returned to the United States, Janene had not had any luck contacting Sa'id's lawyer to see what could be done now that her husband was back.

On Friday, and over the weekend, lawyers and other advocates had visited Glades, as well as Krome, and talked to some of the men. Sa'id had spoken with an advocate from the team about what happened on the flight. There was mention of a possible lawsuit, but no specifics or promises.

The breakfast conversation turned to what was foremost on their minds—their collective fate. It was Tuesday, and the latest rumor had it that ICE would put them on another plane the next day. As the men talked, another Somali man—one of the few who had his own lawyer—joined them at the table. He had just gotten off the phone with his wife, who'd told him that his attorney had been in touch with the lawyers from Miami, including a legal clinic at the University of Miami's law school. There was more talk of a lawsuit being filed to help them.

Sa'id had no way of knowing that both rumors—about the Wednesday flight and the potential lawsuit—were true. Over the weekend, a team of lawyers, advocates, and law students had worked around the clock to file a class action lawsuit by Monday afternoon, in the U.S. District Court for the Southern District of Florida. The lawsuit, *Ibrahim v. Assistant Field Office Director,* was designed to stop the next flight and give the men and women an opportunity to reopen their individual immigration cases, if they chose. Although immigration judges had previously ordered each of the 92 people deported, they still had a right to seek the reopening of their cases for a new hearing. The first named plaintiff was Farah Ibrahim, a diminutive asylum seeker in his early twenties whom ICE's SRT officers had put in a straitjacket for over two hours while the plane was on the tarmac in Senegal.

At the start of the workday on Tuesday, the Clerk of the U.S. District Court processed *Ibrahim v. Assistant Field Office Director* and assigned the lawsuit, randomly, to Judge Darrin P. Gayles, known for a patient and practical approach on the bench. When President Obama appointed him in 2014, he was celebrated by the media as the first openly gay Black federal court judge. Judge Gayles was familiar with the inner workings of the immigration agency. Early in his legal career, he had worked for two years for the federal government as a prosecutor in immigration court. There, he earned a reputation as a decent and fair government attorney. He left his job as an immigration prosecutor to join the U.S. Attorney's Office in Miami—the same office that would defend ICE in the lawsuit on behalf of the group of 92 Somalis.

Judge Gayles arrived at work Tuesday morning to find the newly filed emergency case awaiting his review. Pulling it up on his computer, he and his law clerk read the 33-page complaint, 21-page emergency request and legal argument, and 34 pages of plaintiff and expert declarations. It was a lot to take in. With the flight scheduled for the next day, Judge Gayles would have to act fast if he wanted to intervene.

The names of seven men, three at Glades and four at Krome, appeared as representatives of the entire group—the "named plaintiffs." Farah Ibrahim described in a declaration what had happened right before officers on the plane straitjacketed him, using a constraint called the WRAP but nicknamed the "burrito."

"An officer grabbed me by the collar, and I fell to the floor. Officers began dragging me down the aisle and beating me. The officers kicked me in the back and stepped on my hand. They kicked me in the head. One pushed his thumb hard into my neck below my ear and next to my jaw. I fell unconscious for a few minutes."

Another named plaintiff, Abdiwali Ahmed Siyad, wrote: "The chains were too tight and the guards refused to have them looser. An

ICE guard stepped on my shackles and palmed my face and shoved me down twice. The guards also refused to let me pray or use the bathroom. I only used the bathroom once in front of the guards during 48 hours. I got sick and vomited in the bathroom."

Plaintiff Ismael Abdirashed Mohamed described what happened when he asked to go to the bathroom. An "ICE guard stepped on my shackles and poked me in the eye. My eye is damaged now . . . my vision is extremely blurry, and I still cannot see out of my eye." Officers threatened to "beat the shit out of [me]."

Despite this mistreatment, the lawsuit did not directly challenge the shackling and other physical abuse on Flight N225AX. The legal team had decided that monetary damages for injuries sustained by the group of 92 during the flight seemed less urgent than stopping the looming deportations.

In the lawsuit before Judge Gayles, the lawyers argued that the law—the Immigration and Nationality Act and the U.S. Constitution's guarantee of due process—required ICE to hold the group of 92 men and women in the country until each person was afforded a fair opportunity to prepare, file, and have adjudicated a motion to reopen their immigration case based on changed country conditions in Somalia. They further asked that the men and women not be transferred outside of South Florida so that they could remain near the lawyers. Only a handful of the group had engaged attorneys. The rest had no one else to represent them.

Even though Somalia was dangerous, it would be difficult for the group to reopen their old immigration cases. Each would have to file their own motion to reopen. The rules for reopening were complicated, and the odds of winning reopening were poor. A reopened case was not permission to stay in the country. It just meant a new immigration court hearing on the merits of the case—with all that entailed, including testimony in court, expert witnesses, and documentation of conditions in Somalia. Even though it was a long shot, reopening was the only available pathway for each person to try and stay in the United States.

The first pages of the legal complaint pointed to Somalia's deteriorating human rights situation, along with the increased danger created by international news coverage of the botched December 7 deportation: "The ICE flight never reached Somalia, but the story of the 92 detainees did, riding a wave of press coverage in international news outlets from the *New York Times* to the BBC. This in turn triggered widespread reporting and speculation about the U.S. deportees in the Somali media." The lawyers argued that ICE was responsible for the "extraordinary public attention"—publicity that would put the 92 men and women "in danger of being targeted by the anti-American, anti-Western terrorist organization, al-Shabaab." If permitted to depart, Wednesday's flight would arrive in Mogadishu at the danger's peak. "ICE's abusive and attention-drawing actions on the December 7 flight occurred just weeks after al-Shabaab's massive bomb attack in Mogadishu on October 14, 2017. This terrorist attack killed over 500 people and was a transformative event widely referred to as 'Somalia's 9/11.'" The October 14th attack had prompted the United States to launch bombing raids against al-Shabaab inside Somalia during November. Somalia, according to U.S. immigration officials in Washington, DC, was experiencing "one of the worst humanitarian crises in the world." The escalation of al-Shabaab's terrorist violence, coupled with the U.S. military's retaliation, multiplied the risks created by media coverage about Flight N225AX many times over.

The plaintiffs asked the court to order the government to halt their deportation. As a U.S. district court judge, Gayles had the ability to enjoin the government from going forward with the flight. In lawsuits that seek the halt of illegal action, rather than monetary compensation, asking a court to issue an injunction can be a powerful tool. Some of the most storied cases in legal history—including *Brown v. Board of Education* and *Bush v. Gore*—involved injunctions.

Judge Gayles scheduled a telephonic hearing at 2:30 that Tuesday afternoon. During the 30-minute call, he listened to arguments by both lawyers but directed his questions to the government attorney, an Assistant U.S. Attorney. He questioned how the government could be aware of the abuse allegations on Flight N225AX and yet move to deport the group of 92 without an inquiry. He said, "If a number of people are alleging abuse at the hands of United States officers . . . it seems troubling that the Government, without doing any investigation, would try to immediately [deport] the only witnesses to the abuse. I mean, that just seems fundamentally wrong, no matter how you couch it legally."

Judge Gayles also inquired how much time he had to rule on the emergency stay motion to halt the flight. "Are we talking about an imminent removal? Is in fact the Government seeking to put these petitioners on a plane tomorrow?"

The federal attorney responded: "Yes, that is the plan, Your Honor. I actually do not know the exact time."

Judge Gayles gave the government until the end of the day Tuesday to file a response to the plaintiffs' motion for an order staying the deportation of the 92 detained men and women on Wednesday.

While the telephonic hearing with Judge Gayles was underway, ICE carried on with preparations to move the Somali men and women out of Glades, for the flight, shackling them once more. The lawyers for the group of 92 found out and called Judge Gayles's chambers, prompting the judge to convene a second hearing less than an hour after the first. The government attorney, confused and exhibiting more than a hint of frustration, stated that he had been unaware of any plans to move the group before the next day and that he would check with ICE. He reiterated his understanding that the plane would not take off until Wednesday.

A couple of hours later, the government attorneys filed an eight-page opposition to the lawsuit. They argued that Judge Gayles lacked authority to even consider the claims. In legal terms, ICE's lawyers argued that the court had no "subject-matter jurisdiction." Judge Gayles, in their view, was powerless to stop the flight, even if there were good reasons to do so.

While the second hearing with Judge Gayles was taking place, Sa'id sat eating dinner in Glades, which had been served early. "Hurry up," ordered a correctional officer. The rush to finish what the officers referred to as "feeding" was unusual. Sa'id wondered if this had something to do with the next flight. He wasn't aware that officers had started moving the Somali men and women in groups to the processing unit, where detained people are brought on their way in or their way out. In the processing unit, officers were cashing out commissary accounts, returning people's civilian clothing, and instructing them to change out of the jail-issued uniforms—all signs that ICE was moving the group for a second attempt at deportation.

Sa'id was one of the last taken to the processing unit. By the time he arrived, buses were parked outside Glades, and the group's personal belongings had been piled in. The supervisor in charge gave him an earful. "You Somalis are wasting your time with the lawsuit." Alluding to the fact that law school clinics were behind the lawsuit, the officer added: "A bunch of college kids just want to practice on you." So both the rumors were true, the bad news and the more hopeful possibility, Sa'id thought. ICE was moving them for the next flight, and a lawsuit had been filed.

Sa'id was seated on a bench, about to be shackled and herded to the bus outside the Glades processing unit when a telephone rang. The same supervisor who had warned him about college students "practicing" picked up the phone. His back to Sa'id, the officer asked, "Are you sure?" Sa'id froze, waiting for what would come next. After seconds that felt like hours, the supervisor hung up the phone, turned, and shot Sa'id a narrow-eyed look. He gave the order, "Get them back into their uniforms. They aren't going anywhere today."

At 6:20 p.m. Tuesday, Judge Gayles had issued a three-page "Order Staying Removal Pending the Court's Determination on Jurisdiction." He "enjoined [ICE] from deporting Plaintiffs until the Court determines if it has jurisdiction over this matter." He further ordered ICE to provide the group "with adequate medical treatment for any injuries they have sustained," to "keep [them] within the Southern District of Florida until further order of the Court," and to "provide [them] with reasonable access to their attorneys." Each side was ordered to submit briefs on subject matter jurisdiction.

Still in the processing unit at Glades, Sa'id joined in the cheering. For now, none of them would be boarding a plane. Sa'id smiled to himself and thought, "Thank goodness for those college kids."

# 10 *Jurisdiction*

Miami, Florida

JANUARY 8, 2018

*Subject Matter Jurisdiction: The power or authority of a court to decide the claims in a case. A court must have subject matter jurisdiction over a claim to rule on it.*

FEDERAL PRACTICE AND PROCEDURE, by CHARLES
A. WRIGHT AND ARTHUR R. MILLER

The Wilkie D. Ferguson, Jr. federal courthouse in downtown Miami is architecturally striking. Its glass curves and angles suggest the hull of a ship. Grassy mounds lend an undulating, wave-like feel to the landscape, while blocking vehicles or crowds from the building's perimeter. Constructed in 2007, the state-of-the-art courthouse was built with security in mind.

Judge Gayles's cavernous courtroom, one of 14 in the building, buzzed with excitement on the morning of January 8, 2018. It was jammed with attorneys and other advocates, law students, journalists, and family members of the group of 92, all sitting expectantly. They were waiting for the hearing on subject matter jurisdiction in *Ibrahim v. Assistant Field Office Director.* Although their fate hung in the balance, none of the 90 men and 2 women detained by ICE were present.

The legal team sat at the counsel's table for plaintiffs in front of a low wooden gate—the bar—which separated the spectator seating from the rest of the courtroom. The government's defense team, comprised of lawyers from the Miami U.S. Attorney's Office, occupied the counsel's table for defendants. The tables faced the far side of the room, where Judge Gayles sat at a desk built into an elevated platform—the bench. In front of him, and to one side, were seats for clerks, the court reporter, and the bailiff. Designed to accommodate jury trials, the courtroom also included a witness box and seating area for jurors on the other side. The solemn grandeur of the courtroom fit the occasion. Judge Gayles would be deciding whether the group of 92 people could continue with their claims for asylum or be loaded onto another plane to Somalia. If no jurisdiction existed, Judge Gayles would lift the stay of deportation and permit the flight to go forward. Although two U.S. district court judges in Massachusetts and Michigan had recently decided in similar cases that they had subject matter jurisdiction, no higher court had yet issued a ruling on the question.

Judge Gayles had ample reason to take the question of jurisdiction seriously. Federal judges preoccupy themselves with subject matter jurisdiction because their courts are tribunals of limited jurisdiction. Laws passed by Congress determine which types of claims federal courts have the power to decide. The fact that a federal judge can consider whether they have subject matter jurisdiction at any time, even if no party to the litigation raises it, reflects the importance of this question. As a leading law treatise observes: "The subject matter jurisdiction of the federal courts is too fundamental a concern to be left to the whims and tactical concerns of the litigants."

Jurisdiction defines the limits of a court's authority to consider the legal claims before it. Law students tackle the issue of judicial authority in their first year of law school, when they read the 1803 landmark case *Marbury v. Madison*. That case was decided during the infancy of the country. Widely considered the weakest branch of government, the Supreme Court had no building of its own and convened in the basement of the Senate chamber. During the prior year, the Court had issued only one decision.

The young United States was in the grip of political upheaval marked by sharp divisions between the two major parties of the day—the Federalist Party of John Adams and the Republican Party of Thomas Jefferson. The two parties clashed over the allocation of power between the federal government and the states, as well as over their views on whether to ally more closely with Britain or France. Adams had lost the 1800 presidential election to Thomas Jefferson, but his party still controlled both the U.S. House of Representatives and the Senate. In the final two days of his presidency, John Adams appointed dozens of federal judges and justices of the peace, in a last-ditch attempt to maintain Federalist control over the judiciary. The Senate hastily confirmed the appointments, but not all of the commission papers had been delivered to the new appointees in time, preventing them from assuming their posts. Jefferson instructed his new Secretary of State, James Madison, not to deliver the remaining commissions. One of the newly appointed justices of the peace, William Marbury, filed suit in the Supreme Court, asking that Madison be compelled to deliver his commission papers.

The Court found that Madison had broken the law by blocking Marbury from assuming his duly conferred judicial appointment. But the Court did not order Madison to deliver Marbury's commission papers. The Court's reading of the Constitution did not give it jurisdiction over Marbury's claim. Although the Supreme Court found it lacked jurisdiction to give Marbury the relief he requested, the Court used its ruling to proclaim its own power. The Court stated, famously: "It is emphatically the province and duty of the Judicial Department to say what the law is." The judicial branch, as opposed to the legislative or executive branches, is the arbiter of what U.S. law requires. Today, unlike in *Marbury v. Madison,* a federal judge takes up the issue of jurisdiction first, refusing to consider the merits of a legal claim if the court lacks the authority to decide it.

In the field of immigration law, lawyers have battled over jurisdictional questions for decades. In 1996, Congress passed two laws that sought to limit the power of federal courts to review immigration cases. Since then, courts, including the Supreme Court, have grappled with just how far Congress intended to go in stripping the authority of courts to hear certain types of immigration cases. Government lawyers often file motions to dismiss immigration cases in federal court for lack of jurisdiction. This tactic was the government's first line of defense in *Ibrahim v. Assistant Field Office Director.* As the parties took two weeks to brief the technical question of jurisdiction, the group of 92 could do nothing but wait.

The January 8 hearing on subject matter jurisdiction before Judge Gayles lasted an hour and a half. The government attorneys went first. They argued that three separate federal statutes had repealed the jurisdiction of district courts to interfere with the execution of deportation orders. The most important provision supporting their argument read: "No court shall have jurisdiction to hear any cause or claim by or on behalf of any alien arising from the decision or action by the Attorney General to . . . execute removal orders against any alien under this chapter." The plaintiffs' arguments for halting the planned deportation flight, they said, were claims related to ICE's decision to "execute" the "removal orders" of the Somali men and women.

The government also argued that the law already provides a mechanism for the group of 92 to seek the reopening of their cases and stays of deportation—by filing individual motions to reopen and for stays of removal before the immigration court. The men and women could even file their motions to reopen from Somalia. For the government, a group stay of deportation was neither authorized by law nor even required as a practical matter, as the men and women could file their motions from abroad, after their deportation.

The lawyers for the group of 92 pressed their strongest point—that the U.S. Constitution itself conferred jurisdiction over their claim: They were entitled to meaningful access to the procedure to seek reopening of their cases and that multiple barriers prevented them from seeking reopening from Somalia. The group needed the court to extend its stay of deportation because the regular procedure for applying for individual stays of deportation with the immigration agency was insufficient. The next flight would be gone before the individual motions could be filed, and conditions were perilous in Somalia, making the communication needed to prepare and file a motion difficult, if not impossible. Moreover, the government was partly to blame for the heightened threat faced by the group of 92. Under these narrow circumstances, the lawyers argued, the district court had jurisdiction to halt the flight until the group had a fair opportunity to file motions to reopen—a right provided under the immigration statute and protected by due process under the Fifth Amendment to the U.S. Constitution.

Judge Gayles posed pointed questions to each side. He wanted the plaintiffs to lay out why a group stay of removal from his court would be lawful, given that Congress had repealed jurisdiction over claims seeking to halt the execution of deportations: "It seems like there is a danger, unless it's really an extraordinary circumstance, of just opening the door to district courts getting involved in something that Congress has explicitly said we don't belong there." Judge Gayles then expressed concerns to ICE's attorneys: "For the Government to not give them a reasonable opportunity to file a motion based on changed circumstances, that seems problematic. I mean, the Government, in effect, seems to be trying to deny them a right, which they have under the law."

By the end of the hearing, Judge Gayles seemed convinced by the exceptional nature of the predicament faced by the 92 men and women: "The Government doesn't contest that [this incident] happened, that there is extraordinary international media attention. That sounds like changed circumstances to me. I mean, at least something that should be adjudicated." Judge Gayles noted that he would issue a written ruling.

Still locked up at Krome, Abdulahi found it difficult to concentrate. His repeated experiences of violence and loss, exacerbated by the extended detention, were triggering frequent flashbacks, insomnia, and anxiety. The Somali men at Krome gave him the nickname baxsani. In Somali slang, this word refers to an escaped or absent mind. The one bright spot in Abdulahi's life at Krome was the hour a day he and the others in his living unit were allowed to exercise outside. During recreation, he forgot the violence in his past; his two-year detention, separated from Fardowso and their infant son; and the immediate threat of deportation to Somalia.

Recreation meant soccer. The men in Abdulahi's living unit came from different countries, including Brazil, Haiti, and Honduras, but many of them shared Abdulahi's love of the game. Even though the attack that had killed Ifraah, his first wife, in South Africa had also injured his knee, Abdulahi remained a force to be reckoned with on the field. Most days at Krome, he found himself in his old position— center midfield—working the ball up the field.

One morning, a few weeks after Flight N225AX, Abdulahi took a hard shot, and his knee gave out. As the ball sailed through the goal, Abdulahi collapsed onto the ground, his old injury more painful than ever. His teammates helped him up, but Abdulahi knew this re-injury was worse. He had felt something tear inside his knee, and he could not put his full weight on his right leg. Abdulahi closed his eyes and winced as the pain shot up his leg. He wondered if he would ever play soccer again.

A week later, in the afternoon of January 8, 2018, following the hearing on jurisdiction in Judge Gayles's courtroom, Abdulahi entered the attorney visitation area at Krome on crutches. The lawyers had scheduled a group meeting with the Somali men in the facility, many of whom were eager for news of the lawsuit. Later, one of the lawyers wrote in an email with medical updates from the group: "Abdulahi Hassan Mohumed is on crutches, was told he needs an MRI on his leg, . . . but has not received it."

Abdulahi sat with other Somali men in blue and orange jumpsuits in a large room used for legal presentations, filled with rows of chairs and a table at the front. Like the smaller, attorney-client visitation booths, the room had windows so ICE officers could watch what was going on inside. Abdulahi and the others had been told that the judge had held the first major hearing in the case that morning. The lawyers expressed cautious optimism. There was no way to predict how Judge Gayles would rule, but his questions indicated he was sympathetic to their case.

The conversation turned to the men's individual immigration cases. The plan was to recruit pro bono lawyers—volunteers—to help the men file a motion to reopen their immigration cases. Efforts were underway to match every person with a lawyer. The legal team had samples and would provide training and support to the lawyers. The men were told to be patient. It took time to prepare a high-quality motion with supporting evidence. When the men asked how long, the lawyers just said "months."

Not everyone was excited about the court hearing or plans to find volunteer lawyers to file motions to reopen. At least a dozen men preferred to be deported as soon as possible. After being detained for so many months or years, they were skeptical that the legal case would ever result in their being allowed to stay in the United States. They felt the timeline for preparing, filing, and getting a decision back on a motion to reopen was simply too long to be locked up after what they had already been through. They wanted out, immediately. The lawyers set up a procedure whereby people could opt out of the lawsuit. In the end, 33 of the original 92 would do so.

Eighteen days later, on January 26, 2018, Judge Gayles put the finishing touches on his 14-page decision regarding jurisdiction—whether the case could proceed in federal court so that those who wished to pursue reopening their immigration case could do so. He ruled in favor of the plaintiffs, allowing them to challenge their removal orders. The decision was a major victory.

Judge Gayles's order exemplifies how the U.S. Constitution and the judiciary provide a backstop to the power held by the legislative and executive branches of our federal government. As Gayles acknowledged, Congress had passed a statute eliminating jurisdiction over the group's claims. Nevertheless, he agreed with the plaintiffs and found that the Constitution's Fifth Amendment guarantee of due process preserves jurisdiction in federal court, due to the unique circumstances of the case. Judge Gayles rejected the government's assertion that the 92 men and women could file individual motions to reopen after they were deported to Somalia. He again admonished ICE, finding it "troubling that the Government would seek to immediately re-remove [the plaintiffs] when their claims arose, in great part, from the Government's own alleged misconduct." Acknowledging that the regular motion to reopen process is generally "adequate," Judge Gayles found the procedure "did not provide an adequate and effective remedy for the exceptional circumstances of this case." The changed conditions on which the group's motions to reopen would be based had occurred so recently that it was virtually impossible for the men and women to prepare and file motions to reopen before ICE's next planned deportation. Filing from Somalia was unrealistic, given the danger. Judge Gayles ruled, "Based on the unique circumstances of this case, including the botched flight, the resulting news coverage, and escalation of violence in Somalia, the Court finds it has limited jurisdiction to ensure [plaintiffs] are able to exercise rights afforded to them under U.S. law."

At a visit to Krome on January 29, 2018, the lawyers informed Abdulahi and the others that, with the jurisdictional barrier removed, they were in no danger of being deported before they could file a motion to reopen. All of Judge Gayles's initial orders would remain in place, including the stay of deportation, the ban on transferring the group out of Krome or Glades, and the order that each person receive necessary medical care and access to lawyers. Later, Judge Gayles would grant a further motion certifying *Ibrahim v. Assistant Field Office Director* as a class action. Each of the group of 92 who had not opted out was now part of the lawsuit, whether they were one of the seven named plaintiffs or not. Although the larger group had already been included in Judge Gayles's orders, the class certification meant the case would proceed as an official class action lawsuit under the federal rules.

Judge Gayles's rulings were critical wins. The threat of deportation was gone, for the moment. Still, little changed in the day-to-day reality of Abdulahi and the other men locked up at Krome and Glades.

Still hobbling along on crutches, Abdulahi teared up when he heard about the judge's decision to let the lawsuit continue. Each piece of good news was precious—sustenance for the long journey ahead. He worried, nevertheless, whether ICE would authorize appropriate medical treatment for his knee. As memories of his two years at Stewart Detention Center in Georgia bubbled up—cold, noisy, depleting—he wondered how long he would be in detention this time around. So far, only a handful of attorneys had been recruited to start work on individual motions to reopen for those who wanted them. More than six months would pass before Abdulahi would be able to file a motion to reopen.

# 11 *Contempt of Court*

## Glades County Jail, Moore Haven, Florida

JANUARY TO APRIL 2018

*Contempt Power: Power of a governmental body (such as Congress or a court)*
*to punish someone who shows contempt for the process, orders, or proceedings*
*of that body.*

BLACK'S LAW DICTIONARY

When Judge Gayles delivered the January 26, 2018, victory on jurisdiction, Sa'id was locked up at Glades in solitary confinement, called
the Special Housing Unit, or the SHU. He had been confined to a
small cell in the SHU for more than a month, as punishment for an
incident over a phone call on Christmas Day.

On Christmas day, just over two weeks after the Flight N225AX
had returned to the United States, Sa'id had waited in line at
Glades to use the telephone to call his wife Janene and the kids.
Although Sa'id and Janene were Muslim, Janene had grown up
Baptist and still celebrated Christmas. The common area of the
living pod that housed 93 men, including a number from the ICE
Air flight, looked the same as any other day, but an unsettled
energy filled the room from the men's roiling emotions around
the holiday they would be forced to spend separated from their
families.

Only two of the four telephones were working, so the line was longer than usual. Many of the men were impatient to connect with their families, especially the ones with children. Some men were still in their bunks. Sa'id stood, waiting his turn, his right arm limp at his side. Sharp pain radiated up the arm from his right pinky finger, which he still could not move. He needed a doctor's attention. Two weeks had passed since Flight N225AX returned to the United States, and ICE had yet to bring Sa'id to the medical unit to evaluate his hand.

As he waited, Sa'id wondered if Janene had hidden the presents in the closet until the kids were asleep on Christmas Eve, in her usual way, and if she had cooked her traditional holiday meal of turkey, stuffing, cornbread, and apple pie. Although their finances had become tight since he'd been in detention, Sa'id knew that Janene would have a lighted Christmas tree. He wanted to be on the phone when Janene's boys opened their presents.

At last, Sa'id's turn for a phone arrived. He stepped forward and reached for the receiver, just as another detained man, who was not from the ICE Air group of Somalis, shouldered in front of him and snatched it away.

Sa'id stopped himself a foot from the man. "Hey, I was next. I'm calling my family. I've got a disabled child at home," said Sa'id, trying to be reasonable.

"Fuck your retarded son, I was next."

Sa'id pictured Janene's oldest son, Jailen, in his wheelchair, his head propped up, his body immobile except for his eyes and face. In a split-second decision, Sa'id started arguing. Other Somalis began moving toward Sa'id as a show of solidarity. Two correctional officers reacted quickly, hollering at the arguing men to break it up. The sergeant approached Sa'id with a warning, already brandishing a canister of pepper spray. Sa'id tried to explain the situation. In response, the sergeant pointed the pepper spray canister toward Sa'id's face at close range and pushed down the trigger.

Pepper spray can stop a grizzly bear in its tracks—and the spray is even more potent for humans. The active ingredient, capsaicin, is the compound found in hot peppers. Often deployed via an aerosol can, the spray is designed to disable people, or to control crowds. As the U.S. Court of Appeals for the Ninth Circuit has stated, the spray induces "disorientation, anxiety, and panic" and causes "intense pain, a burning sensation that causes mucus to come out of the nose, an involuntary closing of the eyes, a gagging reflex, and temporary paralysis of the larynx." Dubbed a "poison" by the U.S. Centers for Disease and Control, the substance falls under the category of "riot control agents" that are banned in warfare by the Chemicals Weapon Convention. Pepper spray is, nonetheless, allowed in United States jails and prisons. After an incarcerated individual killed a federal prison corrections officer in 2016, Congress passed legislation permitting federal employees to carry pepper spray in jails and prisons holding people in criminal custody. Almost immediately after Congress authorized this use of pepper spray, reports of prison officials dousing incarcerated people for punishment, or apparent amusement—as opposed to the allowed purpose of self-defense— began to surface.

Unlike the criminal legal system, the civil immigration system authorized the use of pepper spray against detained people decades ago. Under ICE's own standards, when deploying the spray, officers are supposed to emit no longer than two-second bursts, with pauses in between to assess whether the person is willing to submit. Pepper spray is prohibited when a person is less than three feet away, in handcuffs, or in a small, confined space. In 1999, a union representing border patrol agents filed a case protesting the requirement of one-time exposure to pepper spray as part of the training for agents who elected to carry it. The union cited the "very real possibility of short- and long-term health risks and serious adverse effects." The complaint pointed to an army report that cited pepper spray exposure as a possible cause of death of 14 individuals in police custody. Despite these dangers, the officers at Glades routinely use pepper spray, including at close range and in small cells. For years, advocates had written letters of complaint documenting correctional officers' use, and misuse, of pepper spray at Glades.

The close blast of spray sent Sa'id stumbling backwards. The instant burn shot from his eyes and ears to the back of his throat. He was blinded and paralyzed by the pain. "I can't breathe," Sa'id gasped. The room seemed to be getting smaller.

"Shut the fuck up!" came the sergeant's command as he blasted Sa'id with more pepper spray, soaking his red uniform shirt and white T-shirt underneath, turning it orange.

The second officer, nicknamed "Tippy Toes" by the detained men because he walked on the balls of his feet, grabbed Sa'id from behind and put him in a choke hold. Sa'id almost lost consciousness as he was dragged through the door to the hallway. Tippy Toes slammed Sa'id to the floor, face down, with his knee on Sa'id's neck, and cuffed him with his hands behind his back. Another round of spray hit Sa'id as he lay prone and restrained on the floor. "Be quiet, or I'll keep spraying," the sergeant threatened.

Sa'id couldn't see. Couldn't breathe. Every inch of his skin felt like acid was burning it. He felt he could die at any moment. His fear triggered memories of Somalia—being shot at during school and watching men kill his father, not knowing if he was next. The officers forced Sa'id to his feet and marched him down the hall, doing nothing to prevent the blinded Sa'id from bumping into the walls.

"Water," he pleaded. Pepper spray dripped off him as he stumbled forward. Everything hurt. He couldn't stop screaming.

The Glades officer manhandled Sa'id down the windowless hall to a cage-like shower. With a shove, Sa'id was in the shower. The officer closed the barred gate. "Take the handcuffs off. I can't go anywhere," Sa'id pleaded. He needed his hands free to wash off the spray. But only one officer was there. Regulations said two had to be present to let a person out of the cuffs. Sa'id lunged forward to push the shower button with his head. He missed but kept trying. He had survived civil war, his father's death, and his mother's rape. Glades would not break him. Sa'id's head finally connected with the button, but the rush of water made the burn 10 times worse. As pepper spray washed from his hair into his eyes, his eyes, nose, throat, and ears were on fire. He kicked the shower fencing in his rage against this torture.

At last, the officer unlocked the shower and ordered him out. A second officer was now present, allowing the first officer to uncuff Sa'id. Ordered to strip naked, Sa'id took off his clothes and stood there exposed in front of the two officers. An officer tossed him a fresh uniform, but no towel, and then brought him to the jail's medical unit. Still in the throes of the burning, Sa'id pleaded with the nurse, Ms. Gonzalez, to send him to the hospital. "I feel like I am going blind. They used too much spray on me."

Nurse Gonzalez laughed. "This is Glades County. We don't send people to the hospital for pepper spray." Without paying any attention to Sa'id's injured hand either, she motioned to the correctional officer to take him away.

The officer walked Sa'id, back in handcuffs, from the medical unit to the solitary confinement cells. The two-story SHU unit— sometimes called "the hole" at Glades—had hallways lined with windowless cells, measuring 8 x 10 feet. The only furnishings inside each cell were a metal bunkbed and an open metal toilet and small sink.

There were no televisions in the cells, but when the officers kept a slot in the door open, men could stand by the door and peer through the opening to see a television hanging in the hallway.

Other Somali men had come to Sa'id's defense during the telephone incident and were already in the SHU, although the man who grabbed the phone was not. Familiar voices called out to Sa'id, through the vents, in Somali. "Sa'id, is that you? Are you okay?" Despite the shower, orange spray still dripped from Sa'id's hair and into his eyes. He could not stop coughing. The pepper spray had trickled into the most intimate folds of his body. Touching or wiping himself only intensified the excruciating burning. It would take two days for the SHU officers to permit him another shower, and he would not sleep for a week. He never got to speak to Janene on Christmas day.

The next day, the officer in charge at Glades, Kevin Harris, stepped into the SHU. He had heard about the Christmas day incident and wanted to size up Sa'id himself. Tall, middle-aged, with a brown mustache, Harris wore boots that facilitated his cowboy swagger. Everyone called him "Major," as in the military, even though his actual title was Director of Operations. He pulled open the thick metal door to Sa'id's cell and stood in the doorway and looked at Sa'id, who sat on his bunk.

Harris had a reputation among attorneys—and not a good one. Once, he told a group of law students and their professor that he thought federal immigration prisoners were being treated better than U.S. citizens in criminal custody, implying that people in civil immigration custody should be treated worse because they are foreigners. Another time, he emailed a scathing memorandum to the same law professor in response to her concerns about conditions and mistreatment at Glades, calling her concerns "hearsay," "false," and "biased." Within minutes, an ICE supervisor who had been copied on the email called the professor to apologize.

"So you are the one who started the riot," Harris said to Sa'id.

"What riot? There was no riot," Sa'id answered. The incident had been a dispute over a phone. Although things might have escalated, it was a far cry from a riot. Five to 10 days in the hole for what Sa'id did was standard. Instead, Sa'id got three months.

Harris made it personal. "You're going to be here until you fly," he told Sa'id, alluding to the next deportation flight, even though he had no control over whether Sa'id stayed in the United States or remained in immigration detention. That was ICE's call. Harris seemed to think he was all-powerful and untouchable, and Sa'id thought that very well could be right.

When Sa'id got access to a telephone the next day, he called an attorney from the legal team. He told her that he was never going to get out of the SHU.

On December 27, 2017, Sa'id sat shackled in a plastic chair in the windowless room used for court video hearings from Glades. Chains encircled his wrists, waist, and ankles—just as they had on Flight N225AX. Since being confined to the SHU, shackling had become a regular part of Sa'id's life.

Members of the legal team and three volunteer medical professionals, including Dr. Stephen Symes of the University of Miami's Medical School, had driven the two and half hours to Glades so they could examine some of the Somali men, including Sa'id. Officer Harris refused to let the lawyers and doctors meet with Sa'id unless he was shackled. When the attorneys tried arguing that they routinely met with people held in solitary confinement at Krome and that the detained men were never shackled, all Harris said was, "We do things different here at Glades."

Sa'id rested his right hand on his thigh, the metal of the handcuff putting pressure on his wrist. A photograph taken by Dr. Symes shows Sa'id in a red jumpsuit with his head bowed and his wrists and legs bound. Another shows Sa'id's swollen hand.

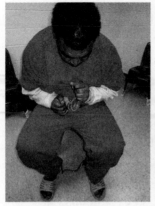

(left) Sa'id at Glades County Detention Center. Courtesy of Stephen N. Symes.

(right) Sa'id's injured hand. Courtesy of Stephen N. Symes.

"Does it hurt?" Dr. Symes asked.

"Very much," Sa'id answered. "I haven't been able to move my little finger since the flight."

Sa'id had initially injured his hand while he was in ICE detention for the first time, during 2015. He slipped in the shower and broke his small finger. The injury had required surgery, which ICE did allow. But after the successful operation, jail officials failed to transport Sa'id to his follow-up appointment with the orthopedic surgeon for removal of the stitches and pins. By the time Sa'id saw his surgeon months later, he had contracted a life-threatening bone infection and ended up hospitalized for weeks. The jail, Boston's Suffolk County jail, had a reputation for shoddy medical care; the neglect of Sa'id's care was just one example. Years later, the ACLU would sue the facility for failure to provide adequate medical care to people like Sa'id.

Glades was proving no better. It had been three weeks since Flight N225AX returned to the United States, yet medical staff at the jail had not arranged for Sa'id's hand to be examined by a specialist.

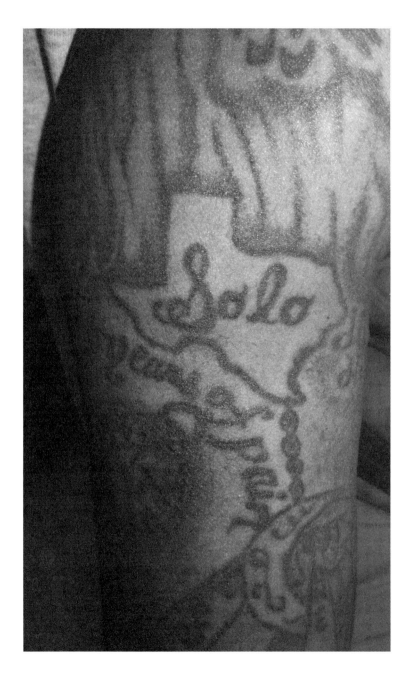

Sa'id's Texas tattoo. Courtesy of Stephen N. Symes.

Sa'id was not the only one whose injuries were going untreated. The lawyers had sent ICE a list of over three dozen individuals from the flight needing medical attention. The injuries included persistent swelling and pain due to the shackling, as well as eye, back, arm, and knee injuries stemming from abuse on the flight.

It is not unusual for ICE to deny medical care to the people the agency has detained. ICE saves money by turning down requests for medical procedures. In 2008, the *Washington Post* obtained an official document in which ICE reported denying requests for medical help totaling $1.3 million "for such things as tuberculosis, pneumonia, bone fractures, head trauma, chest pain, and other serious complaints." Due in part to this neglect of serious medical and mental health conditions, over 200 people have died while in immigration detention since 2003.

Dr. Symes took Sa'id's hand and did his best to perform a physical exam despite the cuffs. "You need to see an orthopedic specialist," he said. He was worried that Sa'id might have nerve damage and permanent loss of function in his hand.

In a January 29, 2018, declaration submitted to Judge Gayles, Dr. Symes wrote:

I examined Sa'id Janale and have also reviewed some of his medical records, including a letter from an orthopedic surgeon who treated Mr. Janale before he was at Glades. Mr. Janale first injured his hand while in immigration custody. . . . He had surgery on his right small finger—an open reduction and internal fixation—with pins placed for stabilization. . . . Despite the hand specialist's instructions for ICE to bring Mr. Janale for a follow-up appointment to remove the pins, ICE failed to do so. As a result of this negligence, Mr. Janale got a bone infection, requiring hospitalization and antibiotics for several weeks. Mr. Janale re-gained use of his hand and, after being released from detention, was able to go back to work and use his hand in his normal work. . . . On the December 7 flight, Mr. Janale's hand was re-injured during the time that the plane was on the ground in Senegal. . . . The X-ray taken at Glades is consistent with Mr. Janale's account of having been re-injured on the flight. . . . When we examined him, he had significantly impaired range of motion, and he was in pain. The standard of care is that Mr. Janale *must* be taken to a hand specialist for evaluation and treatment of the dislocation.

Having compiled a list of the group's medical issues, the legal team decided they would ask Judge Gayles to enforce the court's December 18 order requiring ICE to treat the men and women's injuries. It was one thing to have secured the court order mandating medical care. It was quite another to force ICE to comply with what the court had ordered. On January 17, 2018, the lawyers filed a motion for the court to hold ICE in contempt of court.

Judges can hold someone in contempt for such things as missed deadlines or inappropriate courtroom behavior. They have broad powers to control the actions of the parties and others associated with the litigation. When discussing the many uses of a court's contempt power, a nineteenth-century treatise on American law stated, "One kind of contempt is scandalizing the court itself." Seventeenth-century punishments included cutting off the offender's right hand. Today, the federal rules of civil procedure address how the parties can seek to ensure compliance with the court's orders. One option is for the court to hold a party in contempt, which can lead to monetary sanctions, although judges rarely impose them, especially against the government.

The lawyers invoked Judge Gayles's contempt powers in an attempt to close the gap between what the judge had ordered and what was actually happening at the ICE-contracted facilities. In their motion, the lawyers argued that the government was failing to provide medical treatment to the group of 92 and attached the list of people needing the attention of a doctor. Judge Gayles ordered the lawyers for the plaintiffs and the government to meet and try to resolve the medical issues.

On February 7, 2018, two months after lawyers first reported Sa'id's hand injury to ICE, Sa'id had still not seen a specialist for his hand. Dr. Symes sat at a table in the U.S. Attorney's Office in Miami, next to members of the legal team. When the lawyers read off Sa'id's name, Dr. Symes looked directly at the government attorneys across from him and said, "He really needs to see a specialist. It's urgent." The Assistant U.S. Attorney made a note and moved on to the next name on the list.

The meeting lasted three hours, yet nothing much seemed to change. Over the next six months, the lawyers periodically sent ICE the names of people still needing medical care and asked for updates and records of treatment. ICE did arrange for some people to receive the care they required, usually an X-ray or muscle relaxer, but a number of serious medical issues went untreated, including Sa'id's hand. Five months later, in a moment of frustration and candor, one of the lawyers emailed Dr. Symes and others on the team: "As you all know, we have been begging, pleading, and litigating with the government for months now to get proper medical care for our clients. There is a list of about a dozen who are in really bad shape and I have sent the list to [the U.S. Attorney's Office] two times now. It is clear to me that the three-hour sit down we had back in February was a sham."

After months of back and forth between the group's and the government's lawyers, ICE brought Sa'id to a specialist, who called for an MRI of his hand. Yet ICE never authorized the MRI or provided Sa'id with the surgery that, he would later find out, he had without question needed.

After the Christmas Day incident over his attempted phone call to his family, Sa'id had spent three months in the SHU at Glades. At times,

overcrowding was so severe that two people had to share cells designed for one. The jail officers put Sa'id in with a Somali man from
Flight N225AX who had been living in Iowa. The man suffered from
a mental illness. He refused to shower or eat and spat into empty
socks, talking and laughing to himself. In a nearby cell, a despondent
man from Cuba tried to take his own life.

The Glades officers made isolation especially unbearable for the
Somali men. As Sa'id and six other Somalis detailed in sworn declarations, officers called them "niggers" or "boys" and released pepper
spray into their enclosed isolation cells until they vomited. The two
5-inch-tall slits in the cell doors allowed ICE staff to pass food trays,
conduct visual checks, and cuff people without opening the door. The
slots also allowed them to send pepper spray into the cells while
the doors remained closed. Because the ventilation system carried
the pepper spray from one cell to another, whenever one person or
cell was sprayed, they all were.

Concerned for the men's safety, the lawyers filed an 88-page administrative complaint against Glades in January 2018, with the Department of Homeland Security's Office of the Inspector General,
which provides internal oversight of ICE. The Office of Inspector
General of the Department of Homeland Security started an investigation, and investigators traveled to Glades to interview Sa'id and the
other Somali men in the SHU. But even as the investigators conducted
interviews, Glades officers used pepper spray in the isolation cells.

On February 8, 2018, an attorney from the legal team spoke with
the lead attorney for ICE and expressed concern that officers were
continuing to discharge pepper spray into small isolation cells and
that "someone might die." The lawyers knew the dangers of using
pepper spray in this way. Just a year earlier, Florida prison officials
had killed a man by using pepper spray on him in an enclosed space.
The lawyers urged that ICE transfer the Somali men at Glades to
Krome, where officers only rarely used the spray.

Two Somali men in the SHU, Agane and Fuad, suffered the most. Both were in their mid-30s and had come to the United States with their families as children, refugees of the civil war. On the evening of February 9, 2018, the day after the legal team contacted ICE's attorney to tell them about the dangerous use of pepper spray—and just as the investigators were ending their interviews—the toilets in Fuad and Agane's cells in the SHU stopped working and began to overflow. Excrement spewed onto the floor. The men could not kneel on the floor for their daily prayers. Expected to clean their own cells, Agane asked Officer Smith, a young male officer on duty, for a mop. Officer Smith refused and then grabbed his own crotch and made a rude gesture in Agane's direction. Agane started kicking the door. A female sergeant on duty approached. Agane tried again and asked her for a mop. The sergeant replied, "Why are you asking me? Why don't you ask him?" motioning to Smith. Agane tried to explain, but Officer Smith distracted her, engaging her in conversation. She did not look at Agane. By now, Fuad, Sa'id, and the other Somali men in isolation realized what was happening and started to join in the demand that the toilets be fixed and the cells cleaned.

"Monkeys, stop making noise. Go back to the jungle," said an officer.

The first whiff of pepper spray sent Sa'id into a familiar panic. Not again. As the spray collected in his small cell, Sa'id started vomiting. The wife of a man in the SHU later wrote in an email to one of the lawyers: "They pepper sprayed all the Somalis in [the SHU] last night and punched [a] few of [them]."

The shift supervisor on duty at the time was Lieutenant Mendez, a short, stocky, and bald man in his 40s who had worked with the jail for a decade. At 8:30 p.m., he responded to a call that some Somali men were complaining about the toilets and had been pepper-sprayed in their cells. Lieutenant Mendez joined Officer Smith outside Agane's cell and told Agane to turn around near the door and put his hands through the slot so that they could cuff him in back without opening the door. Agane complied. They cuffed him tight—so tight that circulation was cut off, making the veins of his hands pop out. With Agane restrained, the officers opened the door. Officer Smith pushed Agane's head down and walked him out of the cell, into the hallway outside the segregation unit. Another officer on duty that night, Officer Palladino, acted as backup. When Agane complained that the cuffs were too tight, Smith and Palladino grabbed Agane by the arms, one on each side. "Don't move," Lieutenant Mendez ordered. He raised a pepper spray canister within a couple of feet of Agane's face and let it rip.

Agane screamed. As the pepper spray seared across his face, he felt blinded. Smith and Palladino picked Agane up and slammed him to the ground. Agane landed on his right side, his shoulder, hip, and head taking the brunt of the blow. He lost consciousness. When he came to, he was face down, and one officer had a foot on his neck. The other was kneeling on his back, pressing down hard.

"I can't breathe," gasped Agane, crying. His chest and windpipe were being crushed.

"You, motherfucker, deserve this," said one of the officers, as they shackled Agane. They laughed, making fun of his screams. During the attack, Agane had lost his shoes. He could barely walk due to the injury to his hip. The officers brought Agane to a shower in the processing area. Ordering Agane to kneel, Lieutenant Mendez put his hands around his throat and choked him while cursing, "You motherfucking Somali." He still had the pepper spray canister. "Anything more, motherfucker?"

After the shower, a nurse took Agane's blood pressure and sent him back to his cell. The toilet was working but the feces had not been cleaned up. Agane used some pants and a towel to clean up the soiled floor as best he could. He never got a mop.

Through the vent, Sa'id could hear Agane crying. "Agane talk to me. Are you OK?" Sa'id was really worried. Agane wasn't talking, just moaning. A number of Glades officers were angry about the investigation by the Department of Homeland Security's Office of the Inspector General and seemed to blame Agane. The captain threatened to have criminal charges for resisting an officer brought against him.

Agane later wrote in a sick-call request: "I was assaulted on Friday night . . . I have cuts on my ankles, cuts on my wrists. My shoulders are cut and bruised. My eyes are swollen and red from Sabre Red OC spray directly to my eye. I was kicked, punched; they stepped on my back. I need to see a doctor as soon as possible, please." He wrote in a second sick-call request, "I would like to have a doctor document my injuries, and examine them. I can't see out of my left eye, and it keeps watering from time to time. My right shoulder hurts badly and has been cut. The right side of my head hurts bad, headache that would not go away. I need to see doctor right away."

Sa'id felt he also had to tell someone on the outside that Agane was seriously injured and was not getting medical attention, but the telephone rules in the SHU were different from those for the general population. The men only had access to a phone when the officers allowed it, usually once a day, when the officers rolled a stand with the phone to their cell doors and passed the handset through the slot. Sa'id would have to wait to make a phone call.

On Saturday, the day after the attack, the officers gave Sa'id access to the telephone. Sa'id's hands trembled as he dialed Janene's number. He hoped that Agane was not as injured as he sounded. After hearing what had happened, Janene called the legal team. The details she relayed, together with the earlier email from the wife of another detained Somali man, spurred the lawyer who took her call to email the rest of the team: "This has reached a breaking point. I'm surprised no one has been killed yet."

Later that weekend, attorneys went to Glades to see Agane, who needed a wheelchair just to reach the attorney visitation area. He had a large bump on his head and lacerations across his shoulders and arms. His left eye was red, encrusted with dried fluids. "I think I need an X-ray of my shoulder and hip," Agane told the attorneys. "My shoulder may be dislocated and my hip broken. I need someone to look at my head." Agane was displaying signs of a concussion from the attack. His vision was blurry, his ears ringing, and he had a persistent headache. Despite Agane's condition, the Glades officers had not had any doctor examine him.

The lawyers requested that Agane be brought to the hospital immediately. They also alerted the U.S. Attorney's Office and the ICE officer in charge of the detained immigrants at Glades. Although it was the weekend, both said they would look into what had occurred in the SHU.

On Monday, an ICE officer showed up to check on Agane, who still hadn't seen a doctor. The officer found him curled up under a blanket on the bed in his cell, moaning and noncommunicative. The ICE officer ordered Agane transported to the hospital emergency room, on a stretcher. "He talks tough shit but screams like a girl when being beaten up," was the response of one Glades officer.

Meanwhile, the contempt motion regarding medical treatment was still pending with Judge Gayles. They immediately amended it to include the abuses in the SHU and again asked that the Somali men at Glades be transferred to Krome. Judge Gayles scheduled a hearing two days later, on February 14, 2018. After a discussion of Agane's condition, the judge paused before saying, "my concern is kind of the slippery slope." He added, "I don't know that this is the Court to hear every single complaint about the facilities and bad treatment." The legal team tried to explain how the abuse was preventing the preparation of the motions to reopen the immigration cases. "It's impossible for us to do what we told the Court we wanted to do, which is prepare and file motions to re-open when we keep running into one roadblock or another. We can't access our clients. When we do access our clients, we find them battered and broken." Judge

Gayles acknowledged that the issues the lawyers were raising were "intertwined" but viewed the allegations of abuse as outside the scope of the lawsuit. He believed there was nothing he could do.

When the legal team followed up on their request that ICE move the Somali men to Krome, the government attorney said that they had asked the ICE officers in charge, and their answer was no.

Agane's experience of abuse dragged on. On April 9, 2018, three Glades officers again assaulted Agane, knocking him unconscious, after he asked for a copy of a grievance form he had filed. At the emergency room, doctors found that Agane had suffered another concussion, and his shoulder was dislocated. On April 13, 2018, officials at Glades accused Agane of resisting arrest and called for criminal charges to be brought. Agane was convicted, and after serving a criminal sentence, he was placed back in immigration detention. In total, Agane would be incarcerated by ICE for three and a half years before being deported back to Somalia.

Judge Gayles never ruled on the request that the government be held in contempt of court for failing to provide medical care, or for the dangerous misuse of pepper spray or the physical abuse. Regarding medical care, the lawyers went back and forth with the government for about a year. Some people got the medical treatment they required. Others, like Sa'id, did not. The Department of Homeland Security's Office of the Inspector General found that Glades officers had done nothing wrong during the Christmas Day incident and did not investigate the abuse against Agane in the SHU. Glades officers went on misusing pepper spray in violation of their own regulations. Not a single officer has been disciplined for their abuse of people held in Glades.

# 12  *Motion to Reopen*

## Krome Service Processing Center, Miami, Florida

JUNE 2018 TO MARCH 2019

*To reopen: To review (an otherwise final and non-appealable judgment) for the purpose of possibly granting or modifying relief. A court will reopen a judgment or case only in highly unusual circumstances.*

BLACK'S LAW DICTIONARY

Abdulahi lay in the medical unit of Krome. His crutches were propped against the bed. His right knee was in a brace. After he reinjured his knee in the soccer game in January, ICE had taken four months to authorize an MRI. The scans showed a complete ACL tear. As Abdulahi had suspected, he needed surgery. Five months later, ICE allowed the knee operation.

When the U.S. government renovated Krome in 2007, it built a medical unit the government considered state-of-the-art. The facility claimed to have the latest in medical equipment as well as overnight recovery rooms and a residential mental health unit.

The small recovery room was much more comfortable than the airless, hot, and squalid storage room where Abdulahi had hid for two months after his parents were murdered in Somalia. But the windowless white walls of the medical unit overpowered him in a different way. More than six months had passed since ICE Air Flight

N225AX had touched down in Miami. Abdulahi had no idea how much longer he would be locked up. He hadn't been able to communicate with his wife Fardowso, directly or indirectly, for months. Any calls out of Krome were expensive and dialing Somalia directly from the jail phone system was almost impossible. Abdulahi focused on the positive: "I have a lawyer helping me. The operation went well. Maybe I will walk normally and play soccer again one day."

Like others from the flight, Abdulahi was requesting the reopening of his immigration case to seek asylum, based on the changed country conditions in Somalia. The lawyer who would file the motion to reopen Abdulahi's case had asked Abdulahi to call him to discuss his case.

Immigration regulations contain a comprehensive set of rules describing how people can seek protection from harm in their home countries through the immigration court system. Under these provisions, Abdulahi and the others in the group of 92 could seek to reopen their immigration cases. According to a special rule, people who fear return to their home countries based on a change in circumstances can file a motion to reopen, even if they have already been denied asylum and ordered deported. Described by courts as a critical "safety valve," a motion to reopen must be "based on changed country conditions arising in the country of nationality." The new evidence must be "material" and must have not been available during the prior court hearing.

When it was time to use the phone to call his lawyer, Abdulahi sat up on his bed in the medical unit, rotated 90 degrees to swing his legs to the floor, and maneuvered his crutches to either side of him. Using his left leg and upper body strength, he struggled to a standing position. He could not put any weight on his right leg without sharp pain. The doctor had prescribed rest, lots of it. An officer stood in the hallway, just outside the door. Abdulahi hobbled toward the door and asked to use the telephone. Perhaps the officer had misunderstood

Abdulahi's English. Or something else had put the officer on a hair trigger. For whatever reason, rather than let Abdulahi make a phone call, the officer stepped toward Abdulahi, blocking his path, and pushed him. When Abdulahi told him not to push him, the officer shoved him harder. Crutches flying, Abdulahi collapsed onto his right knee and fell to the floor. Through the excruciating pain, Abdulahi knew that the officer's aggression had undone the surgeon's good work. In just a few seconds, Abdulahi's dream of a speedy return to the soccer field dissolved.

Six weeks later, in August 2018, Abdulahi entered the group presentation room near the legal visitation area at Krome. He was there with the other Somali men at Krome to attend the legal team's group meeting, meant to provide updates and answer questions. A lawyer from the class action legal team noticed his crutches and, after the presentation, asked him how long he had been on crutches and why it was taking so long for him to heal.

Abdulahi explained. The lawyer commented that there might be action she could take against ICE.

Abdulahi replied, "There was a camera, and the supervisor asked if I want to file a grievance against the officer who pushed me. But other officers came to talk with me and said that the officer has a family. If I complained, the officer could lose his job."

The lawyer sighed, casting her eyes down and then up again. "Did you tell the lawyer helping with your asylum case?"

"Yes, I did. But I don't want to get the officer in trouble. He said he would never do it again." Despite his almost three years in the dehumanizing conditions of ICE detention, the light of Abdulahi's humanity had not dimmed.

"I want to ask you about my motion to reopen," Abdulahi said. He was eager to change the focus of the conversation. "My lawyer filed the motion couple of weeks ago, at the end of July. How long will it take for a decision?" The last visit from the legal team had been in early July 2018, over a month ago, and Abdulahi wanted to take full advantage of the lawyer's presence. It was hard for him to wait while other men from the flight—whose lawyers had submitted motions to reopen months ago—had already had their immigration cases reopened and been released from Krome. Abdulahi's friend Ibrahim had filed his motion to reopen in February. Three months later, the Board of Immigration Appeals had granted Ibrahim's motion. In July, Krome ICE officers had released him because his asylum case had been reopened—all before Abdulahi's motion had even been filed. Ibrahim was now back in Atlanta, reunited with his family. Abdulahi felt like he was falling behind.

Abdulahi was not the only one expressing concern about how long it had taken to get the motions to reopen filed. Many in the group had become discouraged by the time in detention and low chance of success. Some men at Glades had written to Judge Gayles asking to be released from the class action. Four wrote: "I gave no one the authority to make me part of this lawsuit. It's a waste of time. I want to be deported to Somalia immediately . . . Nothing against the lawyers and their effort of helping the ones who are in need of this chance."

Logistical hurdles had caused some of the delay in getting the motions to reopen filed. The litigation team and pro bono attorneys were using a central database to organize and share information. The volunteer attorneys received sample pleadings, mentoring, and check-in calls from supervising attorneys every two weeks. But preparing a well-documented motion to reopen is complicated and time-consuming under the best of circumstances. As experts provided by the lawyers had explained to Judge Gayles, the process entailed interviewing the applicant; helping the applicant draft a detailed declaration; gathering supporting declarations from witnesses, including experts; researching country conditions; compiling country reports;

and preparing a memorandum of law to argue why reopening was warranted. These tasks, if done well, took considerable time from a busy attorney's schedule. The pro bono attorneys were helping the Somalis on top of their regular work.

A further complication was the fact that each of the Somali men and women had gone through a prior court proceeding. It was borderline incompetent to prepare a motion to reopen without knowing what had transpired at the previous hearing. ICE had not digitized its documents, so the files were paper and had to be pulled out of storage. The litigation team had taken on the lengthy bureaucratic process of requesting the files and court recordings for every individual's case. At the same time, the team had asked Judge Gayles to order ICE to make the files available. On February 1, 2018, the judge had ordered ICE to turn over the files within 15 days. But the government kept dragging its heels. Government attorneys started sending the files at the end of March and did not turn all of them over until June. Even then, many pages had sections blacked out, making them of limited use in the preparation of the motions to reopen. The government was withholding information they thought was sensitive and didn't need to reveal, even though laws like the Freedom of Information Act favor broad disclosure.

This delay in getting the files was not the only roadblock thrown up by the government. Another was attorney access. In-person visits at Glades had been difficult because of its distance from Miami and the fact that Glades offered no dedicated rooms where attorneys could hold contact visits with clients. The only space for legal visits was a multipurpose room used for video court appearances and a small room used by medical staff and the U.S. Marshals. Attorneys went to meet their clients, sometimes on multiple occasions, only to face long waits, time limits, or other barriers. Neither Krome nor Glades provided detained individuals the ability to make private and unrecorded calls to their lawyers—a breach of ICE's own detention standards. To make matters worse, Glades Officer Harris had shut down the legal team's group presentations to the Somali men. He claimed that the attorneys provoked their clients to protest their treatment at Glades.

The lawyers had asked Judge Gayles for the ability to make private and unrecorded calls to their clients at Krome and Glades. They also requested five contact visitation rooms at Glades, plus the ability to do group presentations. In addition, the lawyers asked to hold private meetings with clients being held in isolation in the SHU, with their shackles removed for the meetings.

On March 9, 2018, Judge Gayles had ordered the government to give the men and women detained at Glades "the ability to engage in reasonable confidential and privileged in-person contact visits and telephone calls with their attorneys that are neither monitored nor recorded." This order specified "contact rooms" at Glades be made available to lawyers—rooms that would allow the lawyers to have physical contact with their clients, as opposed to talking through plexiglass. But Glades would never provide sufficient contact rooms. Group presentations for the Somalis would never be reinstated. Nor would Glades permit private attorney calls.

The amount of time it was taking to file all the individual motions to reopen was not lost on the government. On July 19, 2018, the government attorneys made a "you snooze you lose" argument to the court and sought dismissal of the case. In their view, any class member who had not already filed a motion to reopen had "unjustifiably delayed" filing it. Even those Somalis who had filed motions and were awaiting a final decision, they argued, could not make a case for the stay of deportation to remain in place.

Abdulahi and the others who had opted to remain in detention and fight their case had always faced an uphill battle. Reopening a final deportation order is a long shot, with less than 10 percent of motions granted. Many immigration attorneys can count on one hand the number of cases they have reopened in their career. But against all odds, the victories were rolling in. Not only were many cases reopened, but also some of the Somalis, like Abdulahi's friend Ibrahim, had been released. Among the first people to be released was one of the two women on the ICE Air flight, a single mother with a young son. An immigration judge had reopened her case and terminated court proceedings against her because she had been put in removal proceedings by mistake. The Somali woman had originally been ordered deported because she had a criminal conviction. But the legal team discovered that it was not the type of crime that allowed the government to deport her. In the end, 78 percent of the motions to reopen would be granted and 58 percent of the group that opted to stay and fight their case would be released from detention.

In the presentation room at Krome, the lawyer answered Abdulahi's question about the timeline for a decision on his motion to reopen as best she could. "It depends, usually three to six months. But it could take longer."

"Let's hope it will take three months rather than six," said Abdulahi. He smiled, turned, and hobbled out of the room on his crutches.

The lawyer watched him leave and tried to put a cap on her feelings. She knew what had happened to Abdulahi in Somalia and South Africa and that he had waited months for his motion to reopen to be filed. Months earlier, she had considered taking Abdulahi's case herself instead of assigning it to a pro bono attorney. But she decided she had already taken on too many of the Somalis' cases. Abdulahi's motion might have been granted by now. But now that Abdulahi's motion to reopen was pending, all he could do was wait.

As Abdulahi waited at Krome for a decision on his motion, the lawyers continued to push ICE to provide him with appropriate medical care. He would spend another six months at Krome asking for a knee operation to repair the damage done by the officer who pushed him down. He would never get the operation at Krome, only over-the-counter medication for his pain. In late 2018, a Krome nurse told Abdulahi, "No nurse wants to meet with you because you have too many medical issues."

In March 2019, a year and three months after the ICE Air flight returned to the United States, a Krome correctional officer shook Abdulahi awake in the middle of the night, well before the usual wakeup time. The officer ordered Abdulahi to get dressed and gather his belongings. Abdulahi, confused, asked why. "You're going to Louisiana to be deported on the next flight to Somalia," said the officer.

As Abdulahi scrambled to his feet to comply with the correctional officer's order, the room felt like it was tilting. How could ICE deport him now? What about the order from Judge Gayles stopping all transfers and deportations? Shaking and unsteady, Abdulahi followed the officer to the processing unit, where he knew he would be shackled, again.

The legal team's greatest fear had come to pass. On March 14, 2019, Judge Gayles had dismissed the class action lawsuit. His reasons for dismissing the lawsuit were straightforward. The Somali men and women had asked for a meaningful opportunity to reopen their cases. He had given them over a year—what should have been enough time for all the motions to be filed and adjudicated. The Board of Immigration Appeals, however, had not yet issued decisions on some of the motions to reopen, including Abdulahi's. From one perspective, Judge Gayles's dismissal of the lawsuit seemed reasonable; a year was a long time. The normal processing time for a motion to reopen was three to six months. From another, a year wasn't sufficient for Abdulahi and the other men with pending motions to reopen. It had been almost nine months since Abdulahi had filed his motion, yet it was still pending with the Board of Immigration Appeals.

There was a gap between what seemed reasonable and what was actually feasible—a disconnect between the courtroom and the real world.

The class action case was closed. Because it was no longer pending, each of Judge Gayles's prior orders dissolved. ICE was no longer barred from deporting any of the group who had pending motions to reopen. ICE was free to transfer people out of Krome and Glades. Abdulahi's motion to reopen, like the motions of about eleven other Somali men, had not yet been granted. With Judge Gayles's stay of deportation lifted, there was nothing to prevent ICE from moving Abdulahi to deport him. ICE was now rushing to get Abdulahi back to the jail in Alexandria, Louisiana, and on the next plane to Somalia.

The lawyers had tried to prevent this exact scenario. In a hearing before Judge Gayles on November 20, 2018, the lawyers explained that the Board of Immigration Appeals can take an extraordinarily long time to decide cases and that the timing was beyond the control of the plaintiffs or their lawyers. If Judge Gayles dismissed the case, ICE would immediately transfer the plaintiffs with pending motions to reopen, moving them away from their individual pro bono lawyers and the class action legal team. The class action lawyers urged Judge Gayles to allow more time. They explained that, with more time, everyone would receive a ruling on their motion to reopen and there would be no need for the lawsuit to continue. They urged Judge Gayles to keep the stay in place until all class members had a final ruling. Judge Gayles did not agree, "It sounds like they have now had a sufficient opportunity to file their motions."

In response to the dismissal of the class action case, the pro bono lawyers immediately filed individual emergency stays of removal for each of the dozen men, including Abdulahi, with cases still pending at the Board of Immigration Appeals. The lawyers also called the clerk to urge the Board to make decisions on the stays and, if possible, the motions to reopen.

Within a week, the Board did grant some motions but denied others. Abdulahi was one of the lucky ones. The Board reopened his case, giving him a second shot at asylum before an immigration judge. But he was no longer at Krome, where Somalis with reopened cases, like Abdulahi's friend Ibrahim, were getting released from detention. Abdulahi was in Louisiana, where no one gets released, even asylum seekers with reopened cases. ICE refused to return him to Krome, where he might have been released and would have been near his lawyer. Instead, ICE shackled Abdulahi once more and sent him to the private immigration jail where his asylum case was first denied—Stewart Detention Center in Lumpkin, Georgia. It was there—back at the immigration court with the nation's worst track record for granting asylum cases and with no prospect for being released—that Abdulahi would renew his fight for freedom.

# 13  *Day in Court*

Krome Service Processing Center, Miami, Florida

AUGUST 30, 2018

*A refugee waiver permits a person granted refugee status to obtain lawful*
*permanent resident status notwithstanding a criminal conviction that would*
*otherwise render them ineligible.*

Although he was still locked up at Glades, Sa'id couldn't believe his
luck. A lawyer who worked at a legal aid office, with many years of immigration experience, had agreed to take his case. With her help, he
had filed his motion to reopen on April 19, 2018, four months after the
ICE Air flight had arrived back in Miami. Even though Sa'id was in
Florida, the motion went to the Boston Immigration Court because
that was where Judge Steven Day had originally ordered Sa'id deported, in 2016. Because Judge Day had retired, the court clerk assigned adjudication of the motion to a different judge, Jose A.
Sanchez.

A few weeks later, Sa'id called the immigration court's automated
number from a Glades telephone to check on the status of his motion.
He learned that Judge Sanchez had granted the motion and reopened
his immigration case—overcoming the first major hurdle in Sa'id's
bid to stay in the country. Struggling to control his tears of joy and relief, Sa'id thanked his lawyer and called Janene to share the good

news. "I can't believe it," she said. "I tried not to get my hopes up, but you and this case are all I can think about." They both wept—the weight of long months of emotion released in seconds. It seemed Sa'id would finally get to meet his new baby son, Sa'id Jr.

But a short time later, a second decision arrived by mail. Judge Sanchez had reversed his earlier decision, leaving Sa'id's 2015 deportation order in place. When Sa'id's attorney called with this heartbreaking update, Sa'id's relief gave way to betrayal and despair. He did not understand how a judge could do such a thing. As rare as it was for a judge to reopen a deportation case, it was all but unheard of for a judge to reverse a decision without giving a reason. His attorney, as shocked as Sa'id was, immediately filed an administrative complaint with the chief immigration judge. Before waiting for the chief judge to respond to the complaint, Judge Sanchez—perhaps prompted by the complaint against him—withdrew his reversal and reinstated his original decision to reopen the proceedings, with a hearing to be scheduled in Florida. Because Sa'id was detained in Florida, not Massachusetts where Judge Sanchez was located, the judge transferred the reopened case to the immigration court at Krome. Glades had no immigration court.

Sa'id felt whiplashed by these contradictory rulings. It was hard enough to endure the two days of abuse on the ICE Air flight and the long separation from Janene and the children, not to mention the months of isolation, pepper spray, and witnessing of similar mistreatment of other Somali men at Glades. The unexplained back and forth of his legal case took an additional toll.

The court scheduled Sa'id's final hearing for August 30, 2018, at the Krome immigration court. Sa'id and his lawyer buckled down to prepare. Sa'id's lawyer had submitted over 200 pages of documents to support his case, including letters from Tiffany and Khadija, the mothers of his older children, the medical records of Janene's son Jailen, plus numerous documents on the dangerous country conditions in Somalia. ICE put up roadblocks to Sa'id's lawyer preparing him to testify. Telephone calls at Glades were not private, forcing Sa'id's lawyer to drive over two hours to see him each time. The lawyer met with Sa'id over half a dozen times to get him ready, although sometimes she arrived at Glades only to be told that there was no contact room available. Still, they had even practiced answering questions on cross-examination—the stage of the hearing during which the government lawyer for ICE interrogates the person they are seeking to deport. Sa'id and his lawyer were ready.

In the predawn hours of the day of his hearing, Glades officers woke Sa'id up, walked him to the processing unit, and shackled him in the usual way. Today, an immigration judge would decide if Sa'id would be allowed to stay in the United States with his family or returned to Somalia, a place he left when he was five years old. Sa'id would have to travel two and a half hours to get to Krome.

A correctional officer motioned for Sa'id and the other 16 men who had hearings that day to take off their clothes, down to their boxers, for a strip search, which involved a "squat and cough" to look for contraband hidden internally. After the men got dressed in their jail uniforms again, the officers started herding them toward the transport van. They passed through a secure double door that led outside. The still, muggy air of the Florida summer morning enveloped Sa'id, warming him just the right amount before he stepped into the frigid air conditioning of the white van. He took a seat in back and managed, despite the handcuffs, to buckle the seatbelt. The windows were covered in sheets of metal with small openings so that no one looking in could see them—a jail cell riding the streets, hidden in plain sight.

Just before 8 a.m., the ICE van passed through the high barbed-wire fences surrounding Krome and pulled up outside the processing unit. Still shackled, Sa'id stepped out under a covered area, then shuffled a few yards into the one-story, concrete-block building. There, officers logged him in, unchained him, and locked him into a holding cell with the other men. The white walls of the room had no exterior windows to let in natural light, only an interior pane through which officers could observe the 17 detained men. Sa'id was surprised to see the listed capacity of the room as 25 people, because the only place to sit was a 12-foot concrete bench along one wall. Back in December, he had been in that same small holding cell with over 20 other men the night the ICE Air flight landed in Miami. Now, he sat down and waited. The hearing would not start until 1p.m.

Sa'id's discomfort could not dispel his hope. Despite all that he had endured at the hands of U.S. authorities—the darkest moments of mistreatment on the ICE Air flight and at Glades—the United States had also given Sa'id his life back, saving him from violence, struggle, and hunger in Somalia and Kenya. After 21 years here, the United States was his home. He would put everything into his fight to stay.

A correctional officer arrived to escort Sa'id into the courtroom. Security officers monitoring them via closed circuit cameras buzzed them through a door that led to a windowless hallway with entrances to three courtrooms. Stopping at the second door, the officer opened and held it while Sa'id entered the empty courtroom. They were the first to arrive. In this room, almost nine months after the failed deportation flight landed in Miami, Sa'id was in immigration court for the final hearing in his case.

The courtroom was standard for immigration court. At the far end of the room was another door, behind the judge's elevated desk. On either side of where the judge would preside were seating areas for a clerk and an interpreter. Two tables—one for the government attorney and another for Sa'id and his attorney—faced the judge. Next to these tables a gated wooden railing separated this area, the well of the courtroom, from several rows of wooden benches, used by witnesses, observers, and officers. The courtroom was also windowless. It looked much like other courtrooms Sa'id had seen but was smaller than criminal courtrooms and had no jury box. Immigration court has no juries. Judges alone make the decisions.

The correctional officer instructed Sa'id to sit at the defense table near the front of the courtroom before the officer walked to the rear to take a seat on a bench near the doorway leading to the hall. That hallway not only connected the courtroom with the secure detention area where Sa'id had been in processing, but it also led to the lobby of the detention center, where Sa'id's lawyer and his family waited.

Sa'id, dressed in his red jumpsuit, watched for the others to arrive. He was finally getting his day in court. He had doubted whether this day would ever come.

The courtroom door opened again. Sa'id turned to see his lawyer walk through in a gray suit with a briefcase on her shoulder. A few steps behind her, Sa'id's mother, Maryan, who had travelled from Texas, stepped into the room. She glanced left and right at the almost empty benches before looking straight at Sa'id. She smiled, although Sa'id could see that she had been crying. Janene, holding baby Sa'id Jr., crossed the threshold next. She wore black slacks with a dressy white, black, and gray blouse. Sa'id's brother Mohammed, and one of his cousins, also entered. The family's escort, a correctional officer carrying a sheet of paper with the list of the court's hearings for the day, had been holding the door and was the last to enter. He ushered Sa'id's mother and Janene to the front row of the bench seating, right behind Sa'id. Sa'id's lawyer took the seat next to him at the defense table and gave her client a reassuring look.

Sa'id turned his head to meet Janene's eyes. She smiled, struggling to hold back tears. He wanted to reach out to her and the baby. They were just a few feet apart, but any physical contact—even a brief hug or squeeze of the hand—was against the rules. Maryan huddled small and still beside Janene. Maryan wore a black hijab. She clutched a tissue, bracing herself, not only for the decision about whether Sa'id would be able to stay in the United States, but also for the hearing itself. Sa'id's lawyer had arranged for Maryan to submit a written declaration stating what had happened to the family in Somalia—including her rape and the murder of Sa'id's father—so that Maryan would not have to relive the traumatic experiences on the witness stand. Even so, the hearing stirred up painful memories and emotions.

At 12:59 p.m., a minute before the hearing was scheduled to start, the door at the back of the courtroom opened again, and the ICE attorney walked in with a rolling crate that contained Sa'id's ample file. It was her job to represent the interests of the federal government, which almost always meant pushing for deportation. The ICE attorney nodded to Sa'id's lawyer and took a seat at the prosecutor's table before unpacking her laptop and the file. She plugged her laptop computer into a cable coming from the wall of the courtroom. ICE, as a government agency, had arranged for high-speed internet while the defense lawyers had no internet connection.

Sa'id's focus on his family was interrupted by another door swinging open—this time the one at the front of the courtroom, behind the judge's raised bench. A clerk entered and announced, "All rise!"

Judge Maria Lopez-Enriquez emerged. "Please be seated," she said, surveying everyone in the room. Judge Lopez-Enriquez held Sa'id's fate in her hands. She had been an immigration judge for ten years but only recently started hearing cases at Krome. Like many immigration judges, she had once been an ICE prosecutor, working for the government to ensure people were deported. Judge Lopez-Enriquez had already denied at least one case of another man who had been on ICE Air Flight N225AX. Sa'id wondered what it would take to convince her to let him stay.

As someone who had first entered the United States with refugee status, Sa'id could apply for lawful permanent residency, a green card. But his criminal record meant that he needed a waiver, which functioned like a pardon in immigration court for his crimes. Judge Lopez-Enriquez had the power to give him the waiver, and his residency, if she found he deserved it. Having family in the United States would not be enough. In addition to family ties and hardship, the judge would evaluate the nature of Sa'id's criminal record, evidence of his rehabilitation, his work history, and the danger he would face if returned to Somalia. She would have to find that Sa'id deserved the opportunity to stay in the United States, despite his criminal record.

Once seated, Judge Lopez-Enriquez stared at her computer screen and clicked a button to start recording the proceedings. She announced Sa'id's full name and his A-number. They were now on the court record. Although there was no court reporter in the room, everything said in the courtroom would be electronically recorded, if needed later for an appeal.

Judge Lopez-Enriquez began with a polite reproach of the first immigration judge from Boston, who, two years earlier, had not advised Sa'id that he could apply for the discretionary waiver as a defense to deportation. "The court should have advised you," she said. Next it was time for Sa'id's testimony, the chance he should have had before the Boston immigration judge. Because of a rule that prevents potential witnesses from hearing the earlier testimony of others, Sa'id's family would have to exit and wait in the jail lobby. Sa'id exchanged a last look with Janene before she and his mother, brother, and cousin followed a correctional officer out of the room. Now, it was up to him.

"Please stand and raise your right hand. Do you swear to tell the truth and only the truth?" said Judge Lopez-Enriquez.

"Yes," Sa'id responded.

"Please be seated. Counsel, your witness."

Sa'id sat down in the witness chair, near his attorney. He perched on the edge of the seat, expectantly, his hands clasped in his lap. He looked at his lawyer and nodded. He was ready.

Sa'id's lawyer asked him questions designed to help him tell his story, from start to finish. She helped him organize the way he told it. Sa'id's spoke like any other American. But few Americans could imagine the story he'd lived. His voice broke as he explained how the clan militia men had killed his father and raped his mother. "As they broke the door in, they shot my father, right in front of us, right in front of my brothers and my sister and my mom," he said, pausing. The retelling was difficult, much more so than he had expected. Sa'id continued, allowing himself to be drawn back into the moment his life had changed forever. He was five years old again, looking at his mother before the violation that would mark her for life. He switched to the present tense. "They start pulling my momma's hair and clothes, and my momma told us to run."

Sa'id could no longer hold back his tears. "As I run outside, I see the neighbors I was playing with the day before. They are all laying outside dead, and I'm stepping over them. It was shocking for me to see that, and until this day I can never forget." Sa'id continued. "It affected me ... I had nightmares ... The men took everything from me."

The judge appeared impassive but watched Sa'id closely as he spoke.

Sa'id continued. It would be a death sentence to go back to Somalia, he explained, because the terrorist group al-Shabaab hunts down people who have embraced American culture. "Al Shabab is the government, the police. They can be neighbors. They can be anybody in Somalia. Al-Shabaab is everywhere. They're known for killing people and torturing." Even if Sa'id tried to blend in, he would stand out. "I look different and dress and talk different than other Somalis." His tattoos, forbidden by al-Shabaab, would make his Americanization obvious. Sa'id stretched out his arm, showing the judge and the ICE lawyer his tattoos, "This is the state of Texas and the skyline of Dallas. I consider this my home."

Next it was time for Sa'id to talk about his criminal record. He went over each of the crimes, explaining what happened. His lawyer asked, "Why should the judge believe you won't get in trouble again?"

"I could be facing death right now if I go back to Somalia," Sa'id explained. "I could lose my wife and kids. I have changed since 2015. I haven't gotten in trouble since I met my wife." Sa'id told the judge that he had not had a drink in three years and that he had been working when ICE picked him up. "I know that if I get this chance that I will do it better, to prove it to everyone I love, especially myself. I can't take back the things I did, I regret having my criminal record. I see it's haunting me until this day."

Sa'id started sobbing, "Please don't take me away from my kids. They are all I have." Sa'id talked about his children. "They call me the best daddy . . . I see how it really affects them—me being a part of their life. I'm scared that I'm going to lose them. They need their father. I don't want to be a failure to them." Sa'id explained how he is a father to Jailen, Janene's oldest son who was paralyzed from the neck down. Sa'id used to get him up in the morning, help him dress, give him his medication, and put him on the bus for school. After school, he bathed Jailen and fed him. "I never had the father figure, so I show them the father figure. I do everything for them. They're my life."

Sa'id went on to talk about Janene, who he said "has been through a lot. She was in an abusive relationship and her father died of cancer. Her mother is in and out of the mental hospital and she has no family at all. Everything affects her right now, she has PTSD." Through his tears, Sa'id said, "I love my wife, and she really needs me right now. She has no family. . . . Me and my wife are like best friends. She's my heartbeat."

The ICE attorney asked only a few questions on cross-examination and then uttered words seldom heard in immigration court: "I think we can give him this chance."

The judge agreed. "I'm willing to give you that chance and grant your application. I cannot imagine what you've been through in your life. It has been a difficult and terrible path."

Sa'id abandoned his attempt to control the flow of his tears. The nightmare was over. Nine months ago, he was shackled on a plane bound for Somalia. Today, a judge had ordered he be reunited with his family in the United States. It had taken two years since ICE first put him in immigration court proceedings for Sa'id to have the hearing he deserved. In that time, he had endured two days of shackling and abuse during the botched deportation flight, months of pepper spray while in isolation in Glades, and over a year in immigration detention. Lawyers had spent countless hours on a class action lawsuit, as well as on preparing his individual case. Once the judge and the ICE lawyer had all the facts in front of them, they were convinced to let Sa'id stay. The final hearing had taken only an hour and thirteen minutes.

Now that the testimony was complete, Sa'id's family was allowed back into the courtroom. They didn't know that Judge Lopez-Enriquez had approved the case, but when Janene looked at Sa'id his face said it all, that he was coming home. Smiles mixed with tears as the family watched the judge sign the order granting Sa'id's waiver and terminating removal proceedings. The ICE attorney had waived the government's right to appeal, so the order was final.

Sa'id would not be immediately freed, and he would be released from Glades, not Krome. So Janene and the rest of the family celebrated by going to a Moroccan restaurant. Janene was starving. She had been so nervous that she had not eaten for two days. At the restaurant, the family began to unwind from the experience in court. Sa'id's brother Mohamed, dressed in a polo shirt, was talking a mile a minute, he was so relieved that Sa'id would not be deported. Maryan, seated at the restaurant table with a plate piled high with halal

Sa'id and Janene outside their home. Courtesy of the author.

Sa'id and his children Samira and Sa'id Jr. Courtesy of the author.

meat and vegetables on couscous, looked at Janene and her son Mohamed and flashed them a rare smile. "God *is* good. We didn't even need to testify." Janene smiled back and kissed Sa'id Jr. on the forehead. The nightmare was finally over.

Not knowing if Sa'id would win his case and, if he did, when he would be released, Janene had booked a flight from Miami back to Boston at 6 p.m. That evening, at 8:30 p.m., ICE released Sa'id from Glades. His lawyer picked him up and drove him the two and a half hours to Miami airport. It was too late to catch a flight that evening, so he spent the night at the airport. He couldn't stop grinning. In the morning, Sa'id boarded the first flight to Boston. His hands and feet were free as he walked down the aisle to his seat. As Sa'id exited the doors at Logan Airport, he saw Janene standing at the curb near her car, holding their 11-month-old baby. Sa'id walked toward them, extending his arms to embrace her and Sa'id Jr. As Janene placed their son in Sa'id's arms for the first time, Sa'id leaned in, tears dropping, to take in the scent of new life. He wore the same clothes he'd had on for the ICE Air flight, but everything else had changed. Sa'id Jr. looked up with his wide brown eyes at Sa'id.

Another miracle.

# 14 *Journey's End*

### Stewart Detention Center, Lumpkin, Georgia

MARCH 2019 TO SEPTEMBER 2020

*Firm resettlement is permanent immigration status in a safe country. People who are firmly resettled in a country are not eligible for asylum in the United States.*

In the small town of Lumpkin, Georgia, the private prison group Corrections Corporation of America painted a message on the water tower that serviced its jail: "Welcome to CCA Stewart Detention Center: America's Leader in Partnership Corrections." Small signs lined the drive leading to the jail gate and directly addressed people en route to detention there: "You Are Important . . . To CCA." In late 2016, when the private prison industry came under increased public scrutiny, CCA changed its name to CoreCivic and painted over the water tower message.

In April 2019, Abdulahi felt neither welcome nor important, shackled as he was in an ICE transport van headed to CoreCivic's Stewart Detention Center in Lumpkin. The four-hour flight from Louisiana, followed by the two-and-a-half hour drive from Atlanta's airport had left him tired and hungry. The jail, run by the country's largest for-profit prison company, was all too familiar to Abdulahi. ICE had locked him up here before, from 2016 to 2017, following his initial arrival at the southern U.S. border near Tijuana in late 2015. Now, after the failed deportation via ICE Air and 15 months of detention at Krome, he was back where he had started.

Stewart's 2006 opening was mired in controversy. With the capacity to incarcerate 1,752 men, it was the largest immigration detention facility in the country. Lumpkin is located on Georgia's border with Alabama, 149 miles from Atlanta, the closest major city. Of the 2,741 people in the town, only a thousand are not locked up at the jail. Its size and remoteness speak volumes about ICE's approach to detention: Build big and make it hard for families, communities, and lawyers to help. Once advocates and organizers got wind of ICE's plans to contract with Corrections Corporation of America to build Stewart, they objected, strenuously. ICE went ahead anyway.

Reports documenting abysmal conditions at Stewart—including Detention Watch Network's 2012 report, "Expose and Close," on the worst immigration jails in the country—found nothing positive to say. Detained men are quoted saying that medical requests either go unanswered or are delayed for weeks or longer. Seemingly motivated by profit alone, the private prison company tries to save money by not serving the detained men meat and dishing up rotten or expired food. The men report finding hair, plastic, and insects in their meals. The drinking water is tinged green. Showers and toilets often do not work, and sometimes the water is shut off altogether. Worse, officers inflict physical abuse on the incarcerated men and degrade them with racial slurs and profanity. Abdulahi knew firsthand what it was like at Stewart, having endured it for almost two years before the failed ICE Air flight.

A correctional officer slid open the side door of the ICE van and ordered Abdulahi out. Looking up at the familiar jail, Abdulahi shuffled in his shackles through the back security entrance. He inhaled a last breath of crisp, spring air and entered the building. As the heavy metal doors clanged shut behind him, a chill ran down his spine. The distinctive odor of the place—disinfectant mixed with dirty laundry—sent him back to 2016. It was here that Abdulahi first learned to live the life of an incarcerated person—to do time. It was here that an immigration judge had denied his asylum case. Abdulahi didn't need statistics to know the hard truth: His transfer out of Krome to Stewart meant a second denial of his case was likely. At Krome, he would have had a better shot at asylum or getting released. Stewart is where asylum cases go to die.

Correctional officers brought Abdulahi to the processing unit and clicked open his shackles. He sat on a hard bench, massaging his wrists while he waited to be called for intake and medical screenings. An officer wrapped a plastic ID band around one wrist and issued him two identical uniforms. The officer directed Abdulahi to change out of his civilian clothes, which would be stored at the jail with his property, the few personal items he still possessed: a bag from his trip up the Americas, some papers, and an empty wallet. After a further two-hour wait, another officer escorted Abdulahi to his assigned housing unit. Walking ahead of the officer, Abdulahi took in the familiar surroundings. The floors of the windowless hallways were painted on each side with yellow lines. Abdulahi knew to keep to the right of the line when walking—to stay in his lane. When they reached his living unit, the officer ordered him to stop and used the intercom to ask the central control room for entry. About 30 seconds later, there was a loud click. The escorting officer pulled open the thick metal door, stepped aside, and motioned Abdulahi through. The living unit was just like the one he had been in before—a single room the size of a basketball court, with yellow-tinged walls and narrow slits for windows. A dozen men were lying on gray metal bunkbeds with cot mattresses, all lined up close together, dormitory-style, in the large open area. A dozen other men sat at tables with stools bolted to the floor.

Telephones were positioned at kiosks in the middle of the room. There was no privacy.

An officer assigned a lower bunk to Abdulahi, on the edge of the sleeping area, right next to the tables. Abdulahi unfolded the mattress to make the bed with the jail-issued sheet and thin blanket. Then he sat down and placed beside him on the bed the small bag of personal belongings. He'd been allowed to keep his legal papers and a photocopy of a picture of him and Fardowso on their wedding day. Slim, serious, and sporting a trim goatee, Abdulahi wore a formal shirt and trousers with dark dress shoes. Fardowso had on a full-length dress, her tranquil face framed by a matching hijab. He wondered how long this next phase of his journey for safety would last and what the outcome would be. Was his asylum case really worth leaving Fardowso behind in Johannesburg and the perilous journey from Brazil to the United States? Abdulahi wasn't sure at all anymore. He lay down on the thin mattress and closed his eyes.

Now that Abdulahi's case had been reopened, he would have a new hearing—a second shot at winning his asylum case. But with its own immigration court, Stewart was a deportation conveyor belt, with Stewart judges denying 94.85 percent of all cases between 2014 and 2019. It wasn't just that the immigration judges ordered the deportation of virtually all people who appeared before them. The Stewart ICE officers—who had the discretion to release people while they litigated their asylum cases—also denied almost all requests for release. Abdulahi's move out of Krome, after the dismissal of the class action lawsuit, had not only put him at the mercy of the court with the lowest rate of granting asylum in the country. The transfer had also made it impossible for him to be released while his asylum case was pending. Abdulahi knew that his friend, Ibrahim, and many others, had been released from Krome once their cases were reopened. He might have been released too if his motion to reopen had been granted sooner or if ICE hadn't moved him out of Krome once

Judge Gayles closed the class action case and lifted the prohibition on transfer. At Stewart, Abdulahi would remain detained for the duration, separated from his Miami lawyer, not to mention the other Somali men at Krome, who had become his community.

Abdulahi's first asylum hearing had taken place in January 2017, before the December 2017 ICE Air flight and after he had already spent a year at Stewart. That hearing had been in front of Judge Saundra D. Arrington. Like many immigration judges, she had been a prosecutor before becoming a judge—first in criminal court and then in immigration court. When Abdulahi appeared in her courtroom, she was in her seventh year at Stewart's immigration court. Her statistics matched those of the other judges at Stewart. Records released in 2019 show that Judge Arrington had denied 95.7 percent of asylum cases in the prior five years. In an August 8, 2017, letter to the Acting Director of the Office of Immigration Judges, the Southern Poverty Law Center stated that Judge Arrington "frequently lacked the necessary patience, dignity, and courtesy that professional rules of conduct require of judges in immigration proceedings."

Abdulahi was lucky that he had a lawyer to represent him at Stewart when he appeared before Judge Arrington for his first asylum hearing in January 2017. One of the Somali friends Abdulahi met in South Africa—also a former shopkeeper whose store had been destroyed—was living in Atlanta after being granted refugee status in the United States. That friend made a decent living as a truck driver and could pay the lawyer's fee for Abdulahi.

On the day of that first hearing, Judge Arrington had done nothing to put Abdulahi at ease. The hearing started with something simple—Abdulahi's lawyer double-checking that the court had received his corrected asylum application.

"There's no 589 in here," said Judge Arrington, referring to the asylum application by the number on the form.

"Would the court then take this one?" said the lawyer, offering a spare copy.

The judge had ignored him. "When was your filing deadline in this case?" she asked, although she knew the answer. Abdulahi was not fluent in English, but he knew enough to understand the judge's sarcasm. He feared the case was tanking before it even started.

The lawyer protested, "Your honor, I did send it in. That's what I'm—"

She interrupted him. "When was your filing deadline for this case?"

"September thirtieth."

"September what?"

"Thirtieth."

"What's today?"

Abdulahi couldn't believe the judge was berating his lawyer for something that appeared to be an error of the court's clerk. Is this what U.S. judges were like, Abdulahi had wondered then? He felt like he was back in South Africa, reporting the carjacking to police who refused to take his report and threatening him with deportation.

Abdulahi's lawyer had tried, again, to explain. "I did send it in. But, unfortunately, it looks like it did not make it to the [court] file . . . These are not material changes."

In the end, Judge Arrington accepted the copy that Abdulahi's lawyer had offered. But she did not drop her caustic tone. Abdulahi did his best in his testimony, but the judge made it difficult. She had reproached him for "rambling" and cut off his lawyer's lines of questioning. At the end of that January 2017 hearing, she had announced she would not be making a same-day decision. Again, Abdulahi would have to wait.

A few weeks later, on February 17, 2017, Judge Arrington finally issued a lengthy written decision. Even before he received the document in the mail, Abdulahi knew it was a denial. Days earlier, he had called the court's automated case information line from Stewart. After putting in his A-number and pressing "2" on the phone keypad for the status of his case, a recorded woman's voice informed him that the judge had "issued a decision in his case" and that "the case was denied." Abdulahi had sat at the jail telephone kiosk, receiver in hand, paralyzed by the news. Everything he had endured during the last year—the sudden unplanned separation from his wife and child, the frantic swim to shore from the smugglers' boat in Panama, the eight-day jungle trek that had likely claimed at least one life from his group—it all ended in a few words from an automated message. The automated message reduced Abdulahi's dramatic and harrowing story to nothing. His long journey fleeing for his life toward safety, step by painful step, was not enough to earn him asylum in the United States. Although Abdulahi had known his chances were slim, he had still held onto hope. He was a refugee. He bore the physical and emotional scars to prove he had been fleeing danger and persecution. Why couldn't Judge Arrington recognize that?

The few recorded words on the automated line had conveyed the crushing outcome of his first asylum case. But reading through all of Judge Arrington's reasons denying the case was far worse. Abdulahi's hands had trembled as they opened the large, manila envelope. He sat on his bunk bed, took a deep breath, and started reading. The 32-page decision displayed the anatomy of an asylum denial—a lesson in how to block off each path to victory by picking and choosing only the facts supporting a conclusion that Abdulahi's story didn't line up with the law of asylum.

Abdulahi had been telling the truth, Judge Arrington wrote, but he was not eligible for asylum on legal grounds. His temporary refugee status in South Africa, she said, disqualified him from even asking for asylum. People who have an offer of permanent immigration status in another country are considered firmly resettled and therefore do not qualify for U.S. protection. Even though Abdulahi's refugee status had been precarious in South Africa—he had been forced to pay bribes to renew that status, and he was never given permanent residency—Judge Arrington found that he had been firmly resettled. She wrongly characterized the money Abdulahi had paid as a "fee" rather than a bribe. In her decision, she also incorrectly assumed that Abdulahi could have obtained permanent South African residency, had he wanted it.

Judge Arrington did acknowledge the xenophobic attacks Abdulahi and his first wife Ifraah had endured but then went on to find that "while foreigners in Africa have been victims of racism and violence at the hands of mobs, the evidence in the record does not indicate that the government of South Africa has taken any actions to substantially and consciously restrict refugees within its borders." She further concluded that the harm Abdulahi had experienced was irrelevant because conditions had changed. The South African government, she wrote, "has recently taken steps to protect refugees from xenophobic violence." Abdulahi had testified how the police tried to shut down his shop and deport him because he was a foreigner, and how he could not get a license to run his shop or to marry. Judge Arrington discounted these incidents, pointing to a decision from the Supreme Court of Appeal of South Africa ruling that refugees had a right to apply for a business license. She had focused on the letter of South African law, rather than on the actual facts of the obstacles Abdulahi had faced when he tried to build a life there.

Judge Arrington did not stop with her firm resettlement finding. She had also ruled that the violence Abdulahi and his family suffered in Somalia—the murder of his parents, his sister's rape, his own kidnapping—was not due to their being members of a minority clan. Rather, the attacks were motivated by "general criminality" and financial gain—factors that did not qualify Abdulahi for asylum, which required him to prove persecution because of membership in a particular social group, political opinion, race, nationality, or religion.

She found that Abdulahi had not established that the Hawadle clan actually persecutes members of his clan, the Shiqaal. To reach this conclusion, Judge Arrington relied on a sentence in a country condition report saying that the Shiqaal, like the Hawadle, are subclans of the major clan Hawiye—implying that it was not plausible that there would be violence between Hawiye subclans and ignoring Abdulahi's credible testimony. Further, she maintained that, by relocating within Somalia, Abdulahi could have avoided future harm. She did not view clan-based violence to have been a significant threat in Mogadishu. Abdulahi could have simply moved to the capital city to be safe.

Back in February 2017, reading Judge Arrington's decision, Abdulahi had sat on his bunk in disbelief. How could the judge call his time in South Africa "firm resettlement" when he'd needed to bribe officials, when the police had threatened to deport him, and—most of all—when he was attacked for being a foreigner and his wife was killed? How could Judge Arrington argue that it was not their status as a member of a minority clan that led to his parents' death and his kidnapping? The targeted violence against him was not a common crime. Each word of the decision dissected Abdulahi's life story—converting the brutality he and his loved ones had experienced because of their clan and status as foreigners into mere unfortunate events.

Now, Abdulahi once again languished in Stewart, awaiting a second asylum hearing. He found it hard to believe this next decision would be any different. Judge Arrington, however, would not be presiding in court this time around, as she had retired shortly after denying Abdulahi's case. Instead, Judge Dan Trimble would hear Abdulahi's case. Before becoming an immigration judge, Judge Trimble had served as a judge for the U.S. Army in Fort Benning, Georgia. He also sat on the board of the Western Hemisphere Institute of Security

Cooperation—a school in Fort Benning known for multiple graduates who later became military dictators in Latin America, such as Panama's Manuel Noriega and El Salvador's Roberto D'Aubuisson. Judge Trimble's record of denying asylum cases was similar to Judge Arrington's. Between 2014 and 2019, he denied 93.8 percent of all cases. When Abdulahi learned of the judge's background, he felt it was unlikely that he would be any better off with Judge Trimble.

The theory behind reopening Abdulahi's asylum case was that key facts related to his asylum case had changed since his 2017 hearing. Human rights conditions in Somalia had deteriorated with terrorist bombings by al-Shabaab, and international press coverage of the failed ICE Air flight had raised Abdulahi's profile, making it more likely he would be targeted by al-Shabaab for his association with beliefs and values in the United States. The goal in reopening Abdulahi's case was to persuade Judge Trimble that he now met the requirements for asylum. Abdulahi would have to convey how much he still feared the Hawadle clan militiamen who had kidnapped him, raped his sister, and murdered his parents. He would have to emphasize the control al-Shabaab wielded over many areas of Somalia. Al-shabaab would target Abdulahi for numerous reasons. He practiced Sufi Islam rather than the version of Islam espoused by al-Shabaab, who regularly persecuted Sufi Muslims, destroying their holy places. In addition, Abdulahi spoke English. He was fond of American sports, music, and TV and he did not wear traditional clothing. His first wife had been an atheist. He had had sexual relations before marriage with his second wife. All of these aspects of Abdulahi's identity would make him highly vulnerable in Somalia. Some asylum applicants have only one reason they fear returning to their country. Abdulahi had many.

Because of the prior denial of his case, Abdulahi either had to show that the facts were now different from before or that Judge Arrington had made a mistake. He had to persuade Judge Trimble that he had never been firmly resettled in South Africa and that there was certainly a reasonable chance—the U.S. Supreme Court has required this to be one in ten—that Abdulahi would be harmed if he were sent back to Somalia, based on his clan membership, his Sufism, or his embrace of ideas and cultural practices associated with the United States.

Abdulahi's lawyer had spent long hours preparing his case. The lawyer was able to obtain a detailed declaration from an expert, based in Norway, regarding the high level of threat still facing Abdulahi in Somalia. Addressing one of the findings in Judge Arrington's denial, the expert explained that although Abdulahi's clan, the Shiqaal, had been adopted into the Hawiya, this fact did not translate into protection from the Hawadle subclan, also a subclan of the Hawiya, because conflicts in Somalia often occurred at the subclan level. Moreover, Abdulahi would face harm or death not only because of his minority clan status but also because al-Shabaab would target him, as having come from the United States and as a Sufi Muslim. For all of these reasons, the expert concluded, deportation "will place him in grave danger and will threaten his life." The expert had agreed to testify in Abdulahi's hearing by phone—a widely accepted practice in immigration court—if Judge Trimble would allow it.

Judge Trimble scheduled Abdulahi's hearing for September 20, 2019, twenty-one months after the ICE Air flight landed in Miami and four years after Abdulahi first crossed the U.S. border. Abdulahi was still recovering from a second operation on his knee—the operation to repair the damage from being pushed down by the Krome officer. The medical unit there had refused to arrange for the necessary reconstructive surgery. Once at Stewart, Abdulahi finally had the operation, a full year after the Krome officer had injured him. In the weeks leading up to his hearing, Abdulahi would have liked more time to prepare his case with his lawyer. The pain from the knee surgery made it impossible to focus on preparing his case. What's more, Abdulahi's attorney had fallen ill. The lawyer filed a motion to reschedule the asylum hearing, which Judge Trimble denied. The hearing would go forward as scheduled. The day before the hearing, Abdulahi's lawyer, who was still not well, flew to Atlanta from Miami and then drove the two and a half hours to Stewart.

On the morning of his asylum hearing, Abdulahi was awake early, having barely slept. He stared at the metal frame of the upper bunk overhead. His body was at Stewart, but his mind was back in Africa, once again troubled by horrific memories. His sister Hamdi being raped, while he was powerless to stop her attackers. His parents murdered, and their killers pursuing him. Ifraah injured, with nothing Abdulahi could do to save her. Despondency overwhelmed him. Where could he go? He had no remaining family in Somalia, and he didn't know where his sister was. He'd lost contact with Fardowso. He would never meet their child. These memories and worries tormented Abdulahi every moment of every day. Usually, he could push them down into his subconscious, to get through his daily routine, to cope. But today, he would have to relive the excruciating details, to make them real for Judge Trimble so he would understand the danger Abdulahi faced. Abdulahi's job wasn't just to make the judge think. He had to make the judge feel.

So much depended upon Abdulahi's ability to lay out his case for the judge, to carry the burden of proof that he would be in grave danger if returned to Somalia. The government prosecutor, by contrast, could sit back and pick apart his testimony, along with the written evidence of conditions in Somalia and South Africa. Even though Abdulahi would tell the truth, what if he got nervous and didn't explain it very well, or stumbled over a memory and told it out of order, or forgot a detail? His lawyer had advised him to take his time and be precise, yet also spontaneous. It was important to be specific and include details, his lawyer said. At the same time, Abdulahi should be direct and to the point. He had to listen carefully to every question from the prosecutor but reply with only the information asked for and nothing more. If he didn't understand a question, he should ask for clarification. So much advice, some of it seemingly contradictory, unsettled him. Giving testimony was a skill. It could be developed with a lot of practice—time with his lawyer that Abdulahi was not lucky enough to have. Despite testifying at the prior asylum hearing, Abdulahi would still be a novice in the courtroom today.

It didn't help that Abdulahi would be communicating through an interpreter. He had learned some English since his first hearing, but not enough to tell his story fluently. Even the most skilled interpreters miss words, fail to represent tone of voice, or misplace emphasis. So much of the impact of a person telling their story depends on the delivery, the emotion conveyed by the words—a lot can be lost in translation. Using an interpreter could become like a high-stakes game of telephone. To make matters worse, the interpreter would not be in the courtroom with him but instead working remotely, literally via phone. Abdulahi couldn't stop thinking about everything that might go wrong. He just wanted the hearing to be over.

Sun streamed through the jail's thin-slotted windows, hitting Abdulahi's bunk. He hauled himself up, trying to distract himself with the jail's morning routine—early breakfast, followed by a lockdown during which every detained individual sat on their bunks to be counted, an hour of recreation, and then lunch. He had been through these motions over a thousand times. Today they seemed to take on new meaning. The result of his asylum hearing would mark either the beginning of a new chapter of Abdulahi's life, as someone granted protection—an asylee free to live in the United States—or the end of his journey for protection—his deportation.

When the time of Abdulahi's hearing approached, an officer arrived in the living unit and called out the last three digits of his A-number and "Somalia." Abdulahi followed the officer to Judge Trimble's courtroom, down the hall from where Judge Arrington's courtroom had been. Abdulahi walked with a limp because his knee was still in a brace post-surgery. Although the courtroom, like the rest of Stewart, was only thirteen years old, it felt older, as if it was added to the jail as an afterthought. The windowless courtroom had a low ceiling. Something was wrong with the temperature controls, resulting in the room being either too cold or too hot. As Abdulahi passed through the courtroom door, he saw Judge Trimble, already seated at his desk at the front of the courtroom. The judge silently thumbed through the voluminous tabbed documents submitted by Abdulahi's lawyer and didn't look up when Abdulahi walked in. Abdulahi quietly moved down the aisle between the empty benches. The only audience would be the correctional officer who was his escort. Abdulahi looked at Judge Trimble, seeking some acknowledgement of his presence from the person who would decide his fate. Abdulahi's lawyer and the prosecutor for ICE sat in front of the judge. Although the judge and ICE prosecutor were seated just a couple of yards from Abdulahi and his lawyer, to Abdulahi the distance felt like an insurmountable gulf.

His lawyer turned and smiled, motioning for Abdulahi to take a seat at the table with him. "At least my lawyer is on my side," Abdulahi thought.

"How are you feeling?" Abdulahi whispered as he sat down.

"I'm still sick, but the judge would not postpone the hearing," the lawyer replied. Abdulahi didn't know what to say and wondered what kind of judge makes a case go forward when the lawyer is sick.

Judge Trimble chose that moment to click something on his computer to start the recording. He then announced Abdulahi's name and file number. Abdulahi's final asylum hearing—which would determine whether he could stay in the United States or not—had begun.

As all trial lawyers know, presenting a winning case means telling a compelling story on the stage of the courtroom—complete with plot, theme, characters, and imagery. The law is important, but it is usually the way facts are communicated that wins cases at the trial level. Abdulahi's chance to convey the true impact of what had happened to him in Somalia and South Africa—to tell his complete story—vanished within seconds, as Judge Trimble announced, "to the extent that evidence has already been presented, we don't need to present it." The judge didn't even want to hear the whole story, what he called a "rehash" of the prior hearing.

Judge Trimble had handcuffed the case.

Abdulahi's lawyer did his best within the judge's constraints. He started by making an opening statement designed to summarize why Abdulahi deserved asylum. He led by addressing one of the main points of controversy, "a critical point." "On its face," he said, "Abdulahi's temporary refugee status in South Africa shows that he was given some sort of protection and status, but the exact opposite is true. He enjoyed none of the rights and privileges of South African citizens. He was not allowed to work. He was never issued a work permit. . . . He was forbidden from obtaining a business license. He managed to operate a shop that was unlicensed but was subjected to bribery from police officers. He experienced beatings and lootings. His first wife died as a result of her injuries from the beatings they underwent. He was never permitted to transition from temporary refugee status to permanent status." Characterizing Abdulahi's status in South Africa as temporary asylum status in "name only," the lawyer explained that Abdulahi could not open a bank account, attend public school, freely leave and reenter the country, or even get a license to marry.

The dangers facing Abdulahi in Somalia persist to the present day, the lawyer argued. "The conditions in Somalia since his 2017 hearing have deteriorated significantly. Al-Shabaab controls enormous swaths of the country. If he is repatriated to Somalia, he will certainly face grave danger, and possibly death and torture. He is a Sufi Muslim . . . which is forbidden by al-Shabaab." As someone who "has been outside Somalia for so long, he will be immediately identifiable as an outsider and stranger. He has no family left in Somalia . . . He is likely to be viewed as a United States government spy" by al-Shabaab.

Judge Trimble turned to the ICE attorney to see if she wanted to make an opening statement.

"No, your honor. I waive opening." She did not need to outline any initial arguments; she already knew the government would likely win the case.

Abdulahi looked down at his hands, resting in front of him on the table as he listened to the prosecutor's exchange with the judge. Why did it feel as if everything was stacked against him?

Judge Trimble addressed the issue of whether the expert on Somalia would be permitted to testify from Norway. "I'm going to deny your motion to have him appear by phone," the judge told Abdulahi's attorney. "I don't find that you've shown good cause for needing the telephonic testimony."

Disbelief barely contained, the lawyer asked, "May I respond, your honor?"

"No," said Judge Trimble, blocking the attorney's ability to create a record that might help on appeal. Whether the expert was in Norway or appearing live, such testimony often makes the difference between a grant and a denial in asylum cases. Abdulahi looked up from his now sweating hands and stared at the judge. Why wouldn't he let the expert testify? Didn't the judge want to know the truth?

Judge Trimble moved on, dialing in the interpreter before asking Abdulahi's lawyer to start direct examination of his client. After a few background questions, Abdulahi's lawyer asked a question designed to let Abdulahi tell his whole story. "Can you explain why you left Somalia?"

The judge interrupted, "Is this in the record or is this going to be something new?" He wanted to ensure that Abdulahi would only be testifying to new things, not the full story.

Through the telephone interpreter and within the parameters set by the judge, Abdulahi and his lawyer did their best to describe Abdulahi's fear, "I fear for my life once I step into Somalia because the man who took our property, the man who killed my family, is alive," Abdulahi explained. He went on to say how he feared al-Shabaab, given his political beliefs and Sufi religion. "If I go back to Somalia, al-Shabaab will kill me. I have no protection in Somalia. There's no government that can protect me. There's no family member that can protect me." But Abdulahi needed the judge to understand, on an emotional level, what it was like to be in his shoes. Yet Abdulahi had no opportunity to explain why a central motivation of the Hawadle militia men to murder his parents was their minority clan status, rather than the "general criminality" that Judge Arrington had cited in her decision earlier. When talking about South Africa, he struggled to make the restrictions, the violence, and the police threats real for Judge Trimble.

Abdulahi's lawyer focused on the current threat posed by al-Shabaab. "Do you believe your life would be in danger if you return to Somalia because you have been in the United States?"

"Yes."

"Do you speak Somali with an accent?"

"My Somali accent? I don't speak like I used to before?"

"Is that because you speak good English as well?"

"Yes."

"Would your accent be immediately identifiable as an English speaker if you were to return to Somalia?"

"Yes." Abdulahi then explained why this fact would trigger a threat from al-Shabaab. "If they sense you have an English accent, they immediately assume you are coming from some western country, and they will think you are a spy. They believe western culture is a bad influence."

His lawyer continued, "Do you believe that you would be safe anywhere in Somalia?"

Without missing a beat, Abdulahi answered, "No." He added that, as a Sufi Muslim, he would likely be harmed for practicing his religion and for holding other beliefs antithetical to those of al-Shabaab—such as his conviction that women are equal to men and his belief in democracy and freedom of speech.

On cross examination, ICE's lawyer focused on whether Abdulahi still had refugee status in South Africa. When she suggested that he could have pursued permanent resident status or renewed his temporary status in South Africa, Abdulahi countered, "To renew your temporary permit, you have to go through the hoops. When you get to the Home Affairs office, the security guard in front . . . won't let you in the building."

After the cross-examination, and brief redirect questioning from his lawyer, Abdulahi's testimony was complete. Usually, the next stage would be closing arguments, but Judge Trimble skipped them, instead requiring each side to submit their arguments in writing. Like Judge Arrington before him, Judge Trimble closed the hearing by saying he would issue a written decision later. Abdulahi would have to wait yet again.

He trudged back to the living unit, to his bare existence. He spent a lot of time lying on his side on his bunk, facing away from the common area. An invisible heaviness weighed on him, like someone was pressing on his chest, pinning him down. Judge Trimble's grant rate was no different from Judge Arrington's. Abdulahi knew better than to believe he could win.

On December 11, 2019, almost three months after the hearing and nearly four years into his detention, Abdulahi received Judge Trimble's decision in the mail—a denial. Abdulahi's English had improved so much that he understood every word of the 23-page decision. He shook as he read each sentence. It was almost unbearable to read. The reasoning tracked Judge Arrington's original decision. All of

Abdulahi's efforts, and those of his lawyer, had been in vain. Later, over the phone, Abdulahi's lawyer told him that he was sorry he was unable to persuade Judge Trimble to disagree with Judge Arrington's conclusions. There was nothing to do except appeal to the Board of Immigration Appeals. Abdulahi's lawyer filed the notice of appeal and wrote a brief arguing why Judge Trimble's decision had been a mistake.

In the spring of 2020, while the appeal was still pending, Abdulahi contracted the coronavirus, along with many others with whom he was detained at Stewart. Although the virus had been raging through immigration detention centers across the country, ICE refused to release people. The crowded and unhygienic living conditions, coupled with the lack of soap and initial lack of masks, turned Stewart and other jails into super-spreader venues. With a high fever and the chills, Abdulahi begged for a COVID-19 test and medical treatment. On April 24, 2020, he wrote to the Stewart jail authorities, "I have difficulty breathing, cough and feel pain in all my body. I need test COVID-19 before I die of this virus. Please help. Thank you." Stewart wrote back, "Thank you for contacting the medical department. You were evaluated by a provider on 4/23/20 and did not meet the criteria for COVID-19 testing."

It took six months for the Board of Immigration Appeals to make a decision. Unlike most appellate courts, the Board permits a single judge to decide most types of cases. On June 1, 2020, a Board member dismissed his appeal, agreeing with Judge Arrington and Judge Trimble. Abdulahi ended up with a final order of deportation against him once more.

Abdulahi had been 18 years old the day his sister came running into their mother's shop to tell him about their parents' execution by the Hawadle militia. He had left South Africa when he was 28. He was now 33. He had lost five years of his life seeking freedom from violence, fighting to live in a place where people would call him by his name not his clan and accept him no matter where he was born. Now the United States had rejected him, denying him asylum for a second time. The U.S. asylum system had again concluded that the violence Abdulahi had suffered—while tragic—was not grounds for granting him protection. According to the government's position, he had lived safely in South Africa and could relocate to Somalia's capital, Mogadishu, where he could hide from the Hawadle militia. Abdulahi had fallen into the deep chasm between the protection he so desperately needed and the reality of what the U.S. asylum system would provide.

Still detained at Stewart, Abdulahi was not himself. He'd lost his usual energy and drive to keep busy. He stopped working in the kitchen and declined the daily hour of recreation. During meals, those around him noticed that his mind seemed elsewhere. The Somalis at Krome, two years earlier, had noticed that he was baxsani, or distracted. Now, at Stewart, his change in behavior had become so extreme that even the correctional officers noticed and kept asking him if he was okay. When Abdulahi met over video conferencing with an attorney from the class action legal team, he flashed her a warm smile but then spoke slowly, his voice weak. The dark circles under his eyes made him look older than his 33 years. The attorney couldn't believe how much he had changed since she had seen him last at Krome.

With the appeal dismissed, ICE had the power to put Abdulahi on another ICE Air flight and deport him to Somalia—the place he had fled fifteen years before. His parents and his first wife Ifraah were dead. Abdulahi didn't know whether his sister was alive. He had no money. He didn't know a single person in Mogadishu, where the deportation flight would land. His first son was probably still in Kenya, in a refugee camp, but he wasn't sure and had no way of finding out. The last time Abdulahi had spoken with his second wife, Fardowso, in 2018, she told him that she and their son were going to Kenya. She no longer answered her telephone.

In September 2020, four months after Abdulahi's appeal was dismissed, ICE transported him back to the Alexandria Staging Facility in Louisiana, the same jail he had been in before the December 2017 ICE Air flight. He was once again at the end of America's deportation pipeline, more broken and damaged than when he had entered. Rather than let him be free while he pursued his human right to seek asylum, the United States had paid private prisons hundreds of thousands of dollars to keep him locked up.

On September 17, 2020, Abdulahi was loaded onto another ICE Air flight to Africa. He was shackled again, along with dozens of men and women from his country, strangers. This time, the flight made the full trip, deporting Abdulahi all the way to Somalia—the reverse Middle Passage complete.

After the plane landed in Mogadishu, Abdulahi walked down the aircraft aisle, through the door, and down the metal stairs to the tarmac. The dry heat of the desert filled his lungs. It felt both foreign and familiar. He squinted in the bright sunlight at the dark brown terminal of the airport building, wondering what fate had in store for him behind the dark tinted glass. On paper, he was Somali. But in his heart, he was stateless. Somalia had killed his parents. South Africa had killed his first wife and almost killed him. The United States, despite promising asylum protection to those in need, had rejected him. Five years an immigration prisoner, for nothing.

Abdulahi paused for an officer to open his shackles. He was no longer in irons, but he was not free.

# Epilogue

I sat at my dining room table staring at my open laptop. A chime announced every new email that arrived in the already crowded inbox of my university faculty account. It was 11 a.m. on Sunday, December 17, 2017, eight days after the ICE Air flight had landed in Miami. Emails had been streaming in since my trip to Krome two days earlier to interview some of the men, including Abdulahi's friend Ibrahim. Over a dozen volunteer lawyers had responded to my call for help and traveled to Krome and Glades to interview as many of the group of 92 Somali men and women as possible. The lawyers were emailing scans of notes from the interviews and handwritten declarations from the group—each recounting the same harrowing details of the two-day ICE Air flight.

I was teaching immigration law at the University of Miami School of Law and directing the school's immigration clinic with my colleague Romy Lerner. Students worked on the legal cases of low-income immigrants, usually people ICE was seeking to deport. But I couldn't rely on my students for help at this moment. The fall semester was over, and they were on break or finishing up their exams for the semester.

I had just gotten off the phone with other advocates from around the country, including attorneys from the American Civil Liberties Union. They could send me sample legal pleadings and provide advice, but, understandably, they could not help draft a lawsuit or join it as co-counsel, at least until it was filed. After all, the lawsuit would have to be written and filed in about 24 hours, as the next plane would likely take off to Somalia in a couple of days. It seemed doubtful that the lawsuit would even get filed.

My next call was to Ben Casper, the University of Minnesota Law School professor who had alerted me to the ICE Air flight. Like me, Ben taught an immigration clinic and had experience managing a docket of federal court cases. His clinic had a client who was one of the 92 on the flight. Ben said he would help. He even had a few law students who could assist by creating a spreadsheet to track information about each of the 92 men and women.

Ben recruited Michele Garnett McKenzie of the Minneapolis group Advocates for Human Rights for help with gathering declarations about conditions on the ground in Somalia and the international news coverage of the failed flight. The legal team had to prove that the deportation attempt had heightened the risk to the Somali men and women by raising their profile. Michele reached out to Minnesota attorney Abdinasir M. Ali, who agreed to track down and listen to the news coverage in Somalia of the flight, which had appeared in both print and radio. Also at Michele's request, longtime BBC journalist Mary Harper wrote a 10-page declaration explaining the danger that the group faced in Somalia at the hands of al-Shabaab terrorists. She detailed how the BBC does not authorize trips to Somalia because it is too dangerous. When she had traveled there in her personal capacity, she hired two armored vehicles with no fewer than six bodyguards. She explained that al-Shabaab would become aware of the arrival of the group of deported Somalis and target them as having come from the United States.

As the handwritten interview notes from volunteer attorneys streamed in, we hastily chose seven people to ask whether they wanted to be lead plaintiffs—the men whose names would appear in the caption of the class action lawsuit as representatives of the group of 92. Lisa Lehner and Andrea Crumine, attorneys with the Miami-based Americans for Immigrant Justice, started drafting the part of the legal complaint describing the seven plaintiffs. Many of their colleagues, including Lily Hartmann, Alexandra De Leon, Tatiana Hernandez, Carson Osberg, and Jessica Shulruff Schneider, volunteered to do interviews at Krome and Glades and to obtain handwritten declarations that we could submit with the lawsuit.

Ben and I worked simultaneously on the other parts of the complaint. We watched each other's cursors move across the screen. Although by Sunday evening the document had begun to take shape, at 9 p.m. it was apparent that we needed help if we were going to file the next day. A single text was all it took for Andrea Montavon-McKillip of Legal Aid Service of Broward County to agree to write the class pleadings—the motion and memorandum of law for the lawsuit to proceed on behalf of the entire group of 92, not just the men named as plaintiffs. A class action requires extensive briefing that defines who is included in the class, the facts and legal principles common to everyone in the class, and why the named plaintiffs, and their lawyers, are appropriate representatives for the entire class. Andrea would later go on to represent Sa'id in his immigration court case.

Ben and I worked through the night. We were feeling too middle-aged to pull an all-nighter, but we did it anyway. Morning came, and we still hadn't finished. I tried to control my rising panic.

At noon on Monday, December 18, 2017, I was still writing. I alerted the duty attorney at the Office of the U.S. Attorney in downtown Miami—ICE's lawyers—that we would be filing a class action lawsuit for the group of 92 Somalis and seeking an emergency order to stop a plane. I kept typing.

I didn't know if I would finish in time to have the court read the lawsuit and take action. We didn't know for sure when the next flight would be leaving, but suspected it was the next day or the day after.

My hands were shaking, making it impossible to type.

I drank a shot of bourbon.

It didn't help.

Finally, later that afternoon, around 2 p.m., I filed the lawsuit on the court's electronic filing system. We had written a class action lawsuit in just over 24 hours, a nearly impossible time frame for something so complex.

Emergency litigation, especially a class action, is all-consuming, fast-paced, and at times frantic. The lawsuit for the group of 92 was all of these. We threw together pleadings. We improvised and crossed our fingers. As the litigation progressed, we tapped into expertise in our advocacy community to build out our litigation team. We celebrated when the ACLU agreed to join the lawsuit.

What set this case apart from other big lawsuits was the ultimate goal of helping each and every person who had been on the flight in their individual cases. The class action litigation stopped the next ICE Air flight, provided the time needed for people to file motions to reopen, secured access to the individual immigration files of the group of 92, and established a mechanism, albeit limited, for raising medical- and detention-related concerns. But the key objective was to ensure that every person who wanted to try and stay in the United States got a pro bono lawyer to help with reopening their immigration court case.

Class action lawyers typically focus on winning the class action litigation, either by obtaining a favorable judgment or by negotiating a favorable settlement. The win is the victory in court or settlement, not necessarily how particular individuals fare afterward. But the case for the 92 was brought by direct services lawyers—lawyers attuned to the goals and needs of individuals. Although stopping the plane was a splashy victory to be sure, we counted real success as ensuring that individuals filed their motions to reopen and got released from detention. We felt it critical to turn the opportunity for reopening individual cases into a concrete reality. If we didn't helped each person seek reopening, stopping the next flight would have just meant more time in detention for the group of 92, followed by another deportation flight—an empty victory.

By the yardstick of individual outcomes, the class action lawsuit for the group of 92 was a success. Our efforts freed approximately 40 people on ICE Air Flight N225AX, about two-thirds of those who opted to stay and try to reopen their case. By other measures, however, the case had limited impact. The root causes of abusive ICE Air flights remain firmly in place. Over the last thirty years, political and economic forces have constructed a powerful prison industrial complex in our country. The United States' massive immigration enforcement infrastructure of jails parallels, and works hand in hand with, our system of mass criminal incarceration and transcends both Republican and Democratic presidential administrations.

ICE Air came into being in 2006 under the Bush Administration. ICE detention beds grew from 6,000 in 1996 to over 34,000 under President Obama, earning him the moniker "deporter-in-chief" among progressives. Under President Trump, daily detention peaked at 50,000 in 2019, before the coronavirus pandemic. President Biden, while claiming to inject humanity into our immigration system, has almost doubled the number of people in detention relative to the level during the pandemic and has refused to shut down the private immigration prisons that hold over 70 percent of all people—almost exclusively people of color—jailed by ICE. The Biden Administration continues to contract with private jet companies at exorbitant cost and has not revisited its policy of across-the-board shackling of people during transportation, no matter how long it lasts. Dismantling our massive deportation machinery will take more than a class action lawsuit.

This story, as I have chosen to tell it, compares the ICE Air flight to a slave ship, an extreme metaphor. Although the men and women on the plane were shackled Africans being forced across the Atlantic, immigration judges, usually following rules meant to ensure due process, had ordered them deported. The men and women had food and water and an airline seat—a far cry from the crowded lower decks of a slave ship where people were stripped naked and starved while they were shackled lying down during the months-long journey between Africa and the Americas.

But many of the men and women understood the ICE Air shackling as like being enslaved. And for good reason. They were bound hand and foot for two days, and many were physically abused. Their reasonable demands to be free and to speak with a representative of their embassy, or with someone from the Red Cross, United Nations, or U.S. Embassy, fell on deaf ears. ICE officials lied to them, thinking they could not handle the truth that the plane was grounded on the tarmac due to a crew rest issue rather than a mechanical failure. Officers, and at least one of the nurses, portrayed the men as bestial, noncompliant, and dangerous, using words to describe the men to the OIG investigators like "frightening," "aggressive," and "angry and combative." Without a hint of self-awareness of their own racial stereotypes, officers spoke to the OIG investigators about how African men are "high risk" for being violent and "destroy[ing] planes" during deportation flights. Somalis, some said, are "the worst" Africans.

Senegal's tarmac operated as a space of exception, a no man's land where no rules or laws applied. The ICE Air officers, like overseers, exercised absolute authority over the men and women. For the ICE masters, the experience on the tarmac was a struggle to control disobedient and dangerous people they viewed as less than human. For ICE, the problem was not that the men and women were shackled and trapped for two days. Rather, the problem was the men's uppity reactions to being bound and contained.

The men and women had limited control over their physical bodies but total control of their minds. Their collective speaking out on the tarmac was a protest of their condition, their contestation of the policies and events that had made the extreme dehumanization and abuse they were experiencing possible. But masters deny the legitimacy, and even the existence, of enslaved people's thoughts and demands. In the words of Frederick Douglass, "There must be no answering back" to the master. The Somali men in the back of the plane dared to "answer back." According to the OIG investigative report, the men were "extremely loud and aggressive, demanding to be let off the plane," and making "demands for release, national media and meeting with US Ambassadors." The men "made statements claiming that they were in Africa now and that this was their land where the officers had no authority over them." For the ICE masters, the men's refusal to submit was like the disobedience of enslaved people: infuriating. How dare shackled Black men protest their mistreatment?

The lens of the master/slave relationship also helps explain the failure of the United States to achieve a diplomatic solution. As documented in the OIG investigative report, the officers in charge only elevated the situation to an ICE Assistant Attaché for Removals who happened to be in Dakar at the time. To the OIG investigators, the Assistant Attaché "denied ever requesting that the local [Senegalese] authorities allow the detainees to disembark the airplane onto their soil," stating for some unexplained reason that this request "would have not been logical." The failure to make a high-level diplomat aware of the crisis or to seek disembarkation suggests that the officials involved did not perceive the Black lives at stake as meriting an intervention by the world's most powerful nation, leaving us to wonder whether the outcome would have been different if the shackled individuals had been White people from Britain or Norway.

Anti-Blackness not only played a causal role in the December 7 ICE Air debacle, but it guided the government's actions during the event and the official interpretation afterward. The slavery metaphor sharpens our understanding of what happened and what continues to happen today, as our headlines about the border with Mexico feature immigration officers mounted on horseback rounding up Haitian men, women, and children with whips, preventing them from applying for asylum.

Today, some from the ICE Air flight are still fighting their cases in immigration court, even though more than five years have passed. Sa'id still resides outside Boston, with his wife Janene. He and Janene now have two children together. Sa'id is a busy parent—managing the kids, taking them to day care and out for activities at the local park, while holding down a demanding construction job. Every minute of every day is precious, his life forever changed by his narrow escape from deportation. As we sat outside Sa'id's home in lawn chairs in the summer of 2021, during the pandemic, he pointed to his Samira, his second child with Janene, and told me, "She wouldn't be here if you and the other lawyers hadn't stopped the flight."

Abdulahi's story has no such fairy tale ending.

Abdulahi lost his appeal in the waning months of the Trump Administration. I helped him prepare for deportation to a place he had not been in for 15 years and that was plagued by terrorism, civil strife, and chronic, desperate poverty. He knew no one in Somalia and had no money. His plan was to try and befriend someone on the deportation flight who had connections in Mogadishu. Abdulahi had two main supports in the United States. The first was the longtime friend he had met as a shopkeeper in South Africa—a man whose shop was also burned—a man who, unlike Abdulahi, had applied for refugee status and been granted it, leading to permission to enter the United States. The second was Jane McPherson, a professor of social work at the University of Georgia. She volunteered in a visitation program at Stewart Detention Center, a three-and-a-half-hour drive away from where she lived. She quickly assembled a crowdfunding campaign for Abdulahi and raised enough money to allow him to survive in

Somalia, at least for a time. Abdulahi's friend from South Africa provided invaluable assistance in getting the funds to Abdulahi after his deportation—not an easy task.

After Abdulahi was deported on September 17, 2020, he bought a cellphone in Somalia, and Jane and I set up voice and text communication with him. We exchanged messages and spoke over the next few weeks. He sent a photograph of himself and talked of his plan to get a visa to enter Kenya. He said, with a hint of optimism in his voice, "I will be in touch." But instead he fell silent. Every now and then, Jane and I exchanged emails to see if one of us had heard from Abdulahi. Neither of us had. A year after Abdulahi's deportation, Jane sent a message to me that ended with the simple statement, "I fear the worst."

Thankfully, Abdulahi's story includes another chapter. On January 13, 2023, just four days before my publisher's manuscript deadline for this book, Jane emailed me to say that Abdulahi's friend in Georgia had been in communication with Abdulahi. A few hours later, Abdulahi and I were talking on the phone.

Abdulahi lives in Mogadishu with a friend from his old soccer team in Beledwyne. He was unable to make it to Kenya because of visa restrictions. When he first arrived in Mogadishu, he did not have a stable living situation and was worried about al-Shabaab agents stopping him on the streets and checking his phone for foreign contacts. As a precaution, he deleted my and Jane's contact information from his phone.

Mogadishu continues to be dangerous for Abdulahi. He narrowly escaped being killed by an al-Shabaab suicide bomb in the city in October 2022 that took the lives of 121 people. He was lucky to only suffer minor injuries to his legs. He continues to worry that al-Shabaab will harm him because of his political views and affiliations. The government's police also pose a threat. In February 2021, the police stopped Abdulahi on the street and asked him to name someone who could verify his identity. Because he had no one to vouch for him, the police arrested him. By chance, a soccer friend, an engineer, was doing a construction job at the jail and saw Abdulahi being held as a prisoner. The friend became his guarantor, leading to Abdulahi's release after a month.

Abdulahi was able to track down information about his wife, Fardowso. She is still in South Africa. After their years of separation, she remarried. Abdulahi has not been able to communicate with his sister, Hamdi, but learned that she might be in the Kakuma refugee camp in Kenya—the refugee camp where Sa'id and his family had lived before coming to the United States.

Today, Abdulahi spends as much time as possible inside because of the danger. He helps his friend in his job but has been unable to find employment of his own. His knee injury from detention is still a problem and keeps him from playing soccer. But despite his circumstances, Abdulahi is still a dreamer. He writes: "future plans and dreams are many in my mind."

# Acknowledgments

Some readers have asked me why I, and the other lawyers, advocates, and law students, are not characters. The omission is intentional. Yes, this is a legal story. Readers might expect lawyers to be central. But the legal story in this book centers the most important characters—those who were shackled on the ICE Air flight. This choice is political rather than literary. Lawyers are too much at the center, much too often. My telling shifts the reader's gaze to the true protagonists of this story. What was it like to be on the plane? To be acted upon by lawyers trying to help?

But others have posed the question, so here I will endeavor to answer it. Yes, I, and many other lawyers, were involved. So many that it is difficult to name them all, both because of their numbers and because the frantic pace of the initial mobilization to help the group of 92 left us little time to keep complete records. We had lawyers on the class action lawsuit, lawyers and paralegals doing interviews at the two detention centers, and lawyers representing people in their individual immigration cases. In total, over 125 lawyers and paralegals and 50 law students were involved.

I apologize to anyone I have left out, but I do not want to let an imperfect acknowledgement be the enemy of a good one.

Joining me on the initial filing of the class action lawsuit were Ben Casper Sanchez (University of Minnesota School of Law), Andrea Montavon McKillip (Broward Legal Aid), Lisa Lehner (Americans for Immigrant Justice), and Andrea Crumine (Americans for Immigrant Justice). Later, we were joined by Anand Balakrishnan and Lee Gellernt (ACLU), and Michele Garnett McKenzie (Advocates for Human Rights).

Theresa Dykoschak from the Advocates for Human Rights helped coordinate pro bono attorneys. Trina Realmuto from National Immigration Litigation Alliance took my call over the weekend before we filed the lawsuit on Monday and wrote an expert affidavit for the case, as did Ira Kurzban. Expert affidavits also came from journalist Mary Harper and from Christopher Paul Anzalone, who at the time was a Predoctoral Research Fellow at Harvard University's International Security Program in the Belfer Center for Science and International Affairs. Many thanks to attorney Abdinasir M. Abdulahi for listening to the international news coverage of the ICE Air flight and summarizing it in a declaration. Later declarations came from Sui Chung, Lauren Gilbert, Malee M. Ketelsen-Renner, Fatma E. Marouf, and Carson Osberg. Lawyers who wrote declarations documenting the issues lawyers had getting access to clients at Glades include John Bruning, Katherine L. Evans, and Lauren Gilbert. Other attorneys and advocates integral to the legal team were Jessica Shulruff Schneider, and Lily Hartman. Local immigration attorneys and paralegals who traveled to Krome and Glades to help interview the group before the lawsuit was filed include Stephen Allen, Dominique Berkhardt, Angelina Castro, Andrea Crumine, Tatiana Hernandez, Alexandra De Leon, Maha A. Elkolalli, Laura Kelly, Andrea Montavon McKilip, Carson Osberg, Tulsi Patel, Omar Saleh, and Jennifer Volmar.

Sarah Paoletti and her students at the University of Pennsylvania Law School's Transnational Legal Clinic helped by taking some cases and visiting Glades. Pro bono attorneys who helped with the individual immigration cases of the group include Nancy Aguirre Frankl, Lisa M. Baird, Ana Barton, Stephanie Bedard, Laura E. Besvinick, Nicholas D. Bortz, Diana Bospachieva, James Brand, Valentine Brown, Emily Brummer, Tom Brunemeyer, John Bruning, Tamara Caldas, Barbara Camacho, Jeffery Michael Cohen, Emily Collins, Kirsten Corneliussen, Laura Danielson, Akash Desai, Audra Dial, Paula Duthoy, Elitsa Encheva, Katherine L. Evans, Brendan Everman, Marge Fish, Michael Ginzburg, Cathy Gnatek, Ilana Greenstein, Leo Guerra, Brenda Haberman, Nadine Heitz, Harris Henderson, Sujey Herrera, Sara Jackson, Julian A. Jackson-Fannin, Joseph Kano, Russell King, Alexandra LaCombe, Julie LaEace, Joseph H. Lang, Jennifer Leiva, Ruilin Li, Bill Lundin, Barbara MacInnis, Jonathan D. Magaziner, Derek Maka, Olga Markarian, Aimee Mayer-Salins, Katharyn Ivera Christian McGee, Brittany Michael, Felix Montanez, Rebeca Mosquera, Mai Neng Moua, John Moye, Deidre Murray, Amir Naim, Katherine Obenschain, Kristie-Anne Padron, Jon Polonsky, Mark Prokosch, Karamat Qayum, Sara Ramey, Mahendra Ramgopal, Caitlin O'Reilly Ransom, Sandra Sheridan Reguerin, Joe Reynolds, Cristina Rodriguez, Rebecca Roque, Brian Rosner, Sophia Rossi, Gayle Sarju, Sarha Schultes, Rob

Shainess, Maureen Sheehy, Sandy Sheridan, Sheila Shuhlman, Katie Silva, Sandra Smalley-Fleming, Losif Sorokin, Elizabeth Summers, Daniel Supalla, David D. Switzler, Ray Tiffany, Elise Tincher, Whitney Untiedt, Peter Upton, Sofiya Veljkovic, Sylvia Walbolt, Matthew Webster, Patrick Weeks, Alyson Wooten, Alan Wright, and Ama Yates.

Special thanks to Dr. Stephen Symes, Dr. Adria Jimenez-Bacardo, and medical student Luke Caleb Cadell, who traveled to Glades and Krome to examine some of the men.

The advocacy for the Group of 92 started between the fall and spring semester of the University of Miami School of Law and while my co-teacher Romy Lerner was on parental leave. Once the spring semester started, Romy and the students in the Immigration Clinic started working on the individual cases of some of the people on the flight and supporting the overall advocacy effort. The students are too numerous to list but include Hasan Ajlal, Marguax Bacro-Duverger, Brett Bembrow, Valori Corral, Cecilia Criddle, Edwin Elliott, Michael Ferris, Rachel Fleishman, Ivan Fontalvo, Karl Jeff Francois, Jessica Gomez, Katarina Gomez, Carolina Gonzalez, Megan Jerome, Briana Joseph, Tatyana Krimus, Sandra Lackmann, Isabella Llano, Maria Llorens, Rachel Lopez, Marva Matthews, Kelsey McGonigle, Heather Miles, Elizabeth Montano, Niki Namazi, Sarah O'Niell, Jose Ortega, Andrea Ortiz, Andrea Passarini, Juan Carlos Pazmino Ponton, Angelina Petrosova, David Pringle, Leyana Quintero, Nicholas Rivero, Candelario Saldana, Jamie Shapiro, Robert Sheldon, Tasneem Shraiteh, Juanita Solis, Christine Swanepoel Stevens, Johana Tamayo, Daniela Torres, Bianca Velikopoljski, Rebecca Wasif, and Emily Wasserman. Students from the University of Minnesota helped as well: Alexis Dutt, Mary Georgevick, and Timothy Sanders. Spring break students from Duke traveled to Glades County jail in 2018 and worked on cases. They were Chelsea DeMoss, Duchoang Pham, and Hannah Wyatt.

I am grateful to my home institution, the University of Miami, for taking a chance on me and granting me a humanities fellowship to support this work, even though I had no track record in narrative nonfiction. I owe a deep debt of gratitude to author and teacher Jeannine Ouellette, who drew upon her deep wells of expertise and patience to teach me the principles of nonlegal writing and coach me on my early drafts. Helen Bronk, my friend and former housemate, provided welcome edits, as did one of my law school mentors, Sarah Ignatius. Abdi Iftin helped me make the descriptions about life in Somalia and Somali culture more accurate. My spouse and life companion, Andrew Stanton, read every word. His insights, edits, and questions made the book sharper and truer. Additional readers who provided invaluable comments include Erin Argueta, Theresa Dykoschak, Lily

Hartmann, Andrea Montavon-McKillip, Kathryn Sharpless, Virgil Wiebe, and Gracie Willis. Many thanks to my research assistants, all students at the University of Miami School of Law: Luciana Jhon Urrunaga, Sav Johnson, Tyler Koteskey, Sandra Lackmann, Jose Ortega, and Maria Piselli. Law school librarians Bianca Andersen, Barbara Cuadras, Abby L. Deese, Pamela Lucken, and Robin Schard helped immensely. I express gratitude to Dalgys Estrabão and Rose Dominguez, both of whom kept the home fires burning in the clinic while I took the time to write this book. Finally, I acknowledge the unconditional love and support of my mother, Clair A. Sharpless, who passed away just months before publication.

# Sources and Notes

Chapter 1. ICE Air

The account of what happened on ICE Air Flight N225AX is based on my interviews with Abdulahi, Sa'id, and others in the group of 92 Somalis as well as a 2018 investigative report written by the Office of Inspector General (OIG) of the Department of Homeland Security. The OIG produced this internal report after the legal team called for an investigation into the flight and filed an administrative complaint with the OIG and the Office of Civil Rights and Civil Liberties of the U.S. Department of Homeland Security. In early 2018, the OIG investigated the complaint but closed its investigation without issuing any public findings. My law clinic filed a Freedom of Information Act lawsuit seeking the findings of the investigation, which revealed that the OIG had issued an internal report on December 11, 2018. As discussed in what follows, the report in many ways substantiated the passengers' account of what happened on the flight. However, the report states that the Office of Civil Rights and Civil Liberties "declined" the case "for prosecution" because "the allegations failed to meet the elements of a Title 18 U.S.C. 242 Deprivation of Civil Rights violation."

The definition of ICE Air Operations comes from an August 13, 2020, ICE Air Operations Fact Sheet. The information about the type of jet plane, a Boeing 767, came from a seating chart provided to me by an OIG official who conducted the investigation into what happened during the flight.

Sa'id showed me the painting of the shipwreck scene by his stepfather. The tragedy is chronicled in a March 3, 1991, article in the *New York Times*, "Fleeing to Kenya: Boat Carrying 700 Civil War Refugees Runs Aground—Mass Burial Held." The characterization of the massive bombing in Mogadishu on October 14, 2017, as Somali's "9/11" comes from multiple major news sources, including the National Public Radio story, "Why the Somalia Attack Is Being Compared to Sept. 11," on October 21, 2017.

The description of GEO Group's Alexandria Staging Facility and what happened the night before the deportation flight came from interviews with Sa'id, Abdulahi, and others on the flight, as well as information and pictures on the jail's website. The information about the number of people in immigration detention and the number of detention centers comes from the Detention Watch Network's website. My source for the profit made by the private prison company GEO Group is the 2019 report by Alan Zibel of Public Citizen, "Detained for Profit: Spending Surges under U.S. Immigration Crackdown." This report, and Jeff Sommer's December 3, 2016, *New York Times* article "Trump's Win Gives Stocks in Private Prison Companies a Reprieve" and Heather Long's February 24, 2017, article "Private Prison Stocks Up 100% since Trump's Win" for CNN, discuss the rise in Geo Group stock after the election of President Trump. The background information about the warden at the Alexandria Staging Facility comes from a newsletter published in the first quarter of 2017 by Geo Group, "Geo World: A GEO Publication for Employees and their Families." The warden's name, like many of the names in this book, has been changed.

Leading books on asylum and refugee law include *The Rights of Refugees under International Law* (Cambridge University Press, 2021), by James C. Hathaway, and *The Refugee in International Law* (Oxford University Press, 2021), by Guy S. Goodwin-Gill and Jane McAdam. Immanuel Kant's principle of hospitality is discussed in his 1795 essay "Perpetual Peace: A Philosophical Essay." Allison Lawlor's *"The Saddest Ship Afloat": The Tragedy of the MS St. Louis* (Nimbus, 2016) gives an account of the tragedy that befell the passengers on the M.S. *St. Louis.* The analogy of the asylum system to Russian roulette comes from the book *Refugee Roulette: Disparities in Asylum Adjudication and Proposals for Reform* (NYU Press, 2009), by Philip G. Schrag, Andrew I. Schoenholtz, and Jaya Ramji-Nogales.

The prohibition on the refoulement of refugees appears in Article 3 of the 1933 Convention Relating to the International Status of Refugees, Article 33 of the 1951 United Nations Convention Relating to the Status of Refugees, and the 1967 Protocol Relating to the Status of Refugees. After President Lyndon B. Johnson signed the Protocol Relating to the Status of Refugees, he sent a "Special Message to the Senate Transmitting the Protocol Relating to the Status of Refugees" on August 1, 1968, urging Congress to provide its advice and consent by a two-thirds majority.

A number of Greek myths refer to fetters, including a myth in which Hephaestus crafts a golden chair with invisible fetters and sends it to his mother, Hera, as revenge for her having thrown him down to earth from heaven after his birth. The Bible refers to "fetters" or "bonds" dozens of times in the Old and New Testaments. In the Qur'an, the term "fetter" is often used to describe the bondages of those damned to Jahaannam.

The OIG investigative report states that Hiatt cuffs were used during the flight. A discussion of Hiatt appears in the October 23, 2011, article "Ethical Trade: Best of British Leg Irons on Sale in America," by Fran Abrams and Edward Helmore, in the *Independent*. In 1986, Hiatt started a joint venture firm in the United States called Hiatt Thompson, as reported by Audrey Gillan in her September 8, 2005, article in *The Guardian*, "UK Firm Picketed over Guantanamo 'Torture' Shackles." In 2008, the British company shut down and moved all production to the United States, as discussed in the June 18, 2008, *BusinessLive* article "Infamous Handcuff Manufacturer to Leave Birmingham." The quoted webpage discussing the legacy of Hiatt handcuffs is *The Hiatt Handcuff Brand Re-emerges with Its Legacy of Quality Restraints*, OutdoorHub, dated January 16, 2014. Hiatt Thompson has undergone another name change and is now called CTS Thompson.

The amendment of ICE's shackling policy from "as needed" to across-the-board is described in the 2018 report by Lily Hartmann and Lisa Lehner, *"They Left Us with Marks": The Routine Handcuffing and Shackling of Immigrants in ICE Detention*, published by Americans for Immigrants Justice. ICE's shackling policy appears in the ICE Air Operations September 1, 2015, handbook, "Loading-Offloading Operations," Section I-Restraint Requirements, and references ICE's Use of Restraints policy, Policy Number 11155.1, Section 5.10, effective November 19, 2012. The handbook states that people being deported by plane "will be fully restrained by the use of handcuffs, waist chains, and leg irons" and that "restraints will not be removed for any reason unless approved by the FOIC or the Assistant FOIC [Flight Officer in Charge]." The referenced Emory University School of Medicine medical study on the effects of handcuffing is "A Prospective Study of Handcuff Neuropathies" and appears in the June 2000 issue of *Muscle & Nerve*. The quoted 2015 medical study is by John Jason Payne-James, titled "Restraint Techniques, Injuries, and Death: Handcuffs," and appears in the *Encyclopedia of Forensic and Legal Medicine*.

Much of the information on ICE Air and its affiliation with Omni Air comes from the University of Washington Center for Human Rights' 2019 report *Hidden in Plain Sight: ICE Air and the Machinery of Mass Deportation*. The quotes and statistics are from government documents cited in the report.

Stig Jarle Hansen of the Institute of International, Environmental, and Development Studies at the Norwegian University of Life Sciences has written about the rise of al-Shabaab in Somalia in his book *Al-Shabaab in Somalia: The History and Ideology of a Militant Islamist Group*, 2005–2012 (Hurst, 2013). He was also the country condition expert who was not permitted to testify in Abdulahi's final asylum hearing, described in chapter 14.

The information about men being placed in spit masks as a show of force during boarding came from the men themselves. The use of masks was confirmed in the OIG's investigative report. During an interview with OIG investigators that took place on January 11, 2018, the Lead Special Response Team Tactical Supervisor for ICE is reported as stating that there were "approximately ten" men put in masks for boarding for "just 'running their mouths.'"

## Chapter 2. On the Tarmac

My research assistant Luciana Jhon Urranga, a University of Miami School of Law student, discovered that the day the ICE Air flight landed in Dakar, Senegal, was the same day of the airport's opening. The inauguration event is chronicled in the December 7, 2017, *New York Times* article "Senegal Opens Airport in Bid to Jump-Start Economy," by Jaime Yaya Barry and Dionne Searcey.

Abdulahi, Sa'id, and others on the flight stated that ICE told them they were grounded in Senegal because they were waiting for a part to be flown from the United States to fix the plane rather than because the relief crew was not sufficiently rested. This lie was confirmed in the OIG's investigative report. The ICE officer in charge is reported to have told investigators that the lie was meant to keep the passengers calm.

The U.S. Department of State travel warnings came from its website. The Senegalese online newspaper accounts of the grounded ICE Air flight are (1) Par Kaolack Infos, "AIBD: 92 Somaliens Expulsés des USA Ont Été Enfermés et Maltraités dans un Avion," Kaolack Infos. *KLINFOS*, May 16, 2018; and (2) Ayoba Faye, "AIBD: 92 Somaliens Expulsés des USA Maltraités et Forcés à Uriner sur Eux-Mêmes dans un Avion le Jour de L'inauguration," *PressAfrik,* December 21, 2017.

## Chapter 3. Civil War

My sources discussing the history of Somalia, including colonialism and the civil war, include the essays in *Putting the Cart before the Horse: Contested Nationalism and the Crisis of the Nation-State in Somalia* (Red Sea Press, 2004), edited by Abdi

Mohamed Kusow; Raphael Chijioke Njoku's *The History of Somalia (The Green-wood Histories of the Modern Nations)* (Greenwood, 2013); *The Invention of Somalia* (Red Sea Press, 1995), edited by Ali Jimale Ahmed; Abdurahman Abdullahi's *Making Sense of Somali History* (Adonis & Abbey, 2017–18); and *Area Handbook for Somalia* (U.S. Department of Defense, 1977), by Irving Kaplan. The quote from Imaan Daahir Saalax about the legacy of colonialism comes from his October 6, 2009, blog post "The Colonial Impact on Somali Politics," appearing in the blog *Somalia Online*. It is also referenced in Raphael Njoku's book. The quote explaining the meaning of loo-maa-oyayaasha comes from Abdi Mohamed Kusow, in chapter 1 of the collection of essays he edited, *Putting the Cart before the Horse*.

In addition to my interviews with Sa'id, I drew on civil war experiences documented in the first-person accounts of women in *Somalia—The Untold Story: The War through the Eyes of Somali Women* (CIIR and Pluto, 2004), edited by Judy El Bushra and Judith Gardner. This compelling collection of essays by Somali women documents experiences similar to those endured by Sa'id and his family, including his mother's rape. An essay by Fowzia Musse in the collection titled "War Crimes against Women and Girls" describes how women in the Kismayo area who were not members of a clan bore the brunt of civil war violence.

Information about the Kenyan Dadaab camp came from Sa'id as well as Ben Rawlence's *City of Thorns: Nine Lives in the World's Largest Refugee Camp* (Picador, 2016) and Cindy Horst's *Transnational Nomads: How Somalis Cope with Refugee Life in the Dadaab Camps of Kenya* (Berghahn, 2006). My sources regarding the Kakuma camp are interviews with Sa'id and Bram J. Jansen's book *Kakuma Refugee Camp: Humanitarian Urbanism in Kenya's Accidental City* (Zed, 2018).

Both Sa'id and Abdulahi talked about the kinky versus soft hair distinction in Somali culture. Information about the clan, caste, and racial distinctions in Somalia also comes from Abdi Mohamed Kusow's "Contested Narratives and the Crisis of the Nation-State in Somalia: A Prolegomenon," which is chapter 1 of Kusow's edited volume *Putting the Cart before the Horse*; as well as Michael M. Phillips's Associated Press February 13, 1994, article, "Racism in Somalia: Arabic 'Soft-Hairs' Always Run the Show"; and Markus V. Hoehne's "Continuities and Changes Regarding Minorities In Somalia," published in vol. 38, no. 5 (2015) of *Ethnic and Racial Studies*. In her book *Making Refuge: Somali Bantu Refugees and Lewiston, Maine* (Duke University Press, 2016), Catherine Besteman also discusses the racialized soft and hard hair distinction. Catherine Besteman's chapter "The Invention of Gosha: Slavery, Colonialism and Stigma in Somali History," in *The Invention of Somalia*, edited by Ali Jimale Ahmed, also discusses the soft versus hard hair distinction.

My sources for information about corporal punishment in U.S. schools are *Corporal Punishment in U.S. Public Schools: Legal Precedents, Current Practices, and Future Policy* (Springer, 2015), by Elizabeth T. Gershoff, Kelly M. Purtell, and Igor Holas, and the 2007 report by Human Rights Watch, *Corporal Punishment of Children in U.S. Public School*. The statistic about how many children were victims of corporal punishment in Texas in 2000 comes from David M. Hargrove's 2011 dissertation, "The American School Discipline Debate and the Persistence of Corporal Punishment in Southern Public Schools," available from the University of Mississippi's Electronic Theses and Dissertations. The Brookings Institution published a January 14, 2016, report on the disparate impact of school corporal punishment on Black children: Dick Startz, *Schools, Black Children, and Corporal Punishment*.

### Chapter 4. Shiqaal Subclan

Abdulahi's backstory in Somalia, and the information about his parents and sister, came from my interviews of Abdulahi. My sources for information about the Sufi sect of Islam are Abdulahi and Alexander Knysh's *Sufism: A New History of Islamic Mysticism* (Princeton University Press, 2017). The quote about the traditional occupations of the Madhiban (Midgan) caste comes from Markus V. Hoehne's "Continuities and Changes Regarding Minorities in Somalia," published in vol. 38, no. 5 (2015) of *Ethnic and Racial Studies*. Hoehne's article cites a 1904 article by John William Kirk, "The Yibirs and Midgaans of Somaliland—Their Traditions and Dialects," in the *Journal of the Royal African Society*, and Virginia Luling's 1984 article "The Other Somali: Minority Groups in Traditional Somali Society," in *Proceedings of the Second International Congress of Somali Studies*, vol. 4 (Studies in Humanities and Natural Sciences), edited by Thomas Labahn. My source for information about the history of slavery in Somalia is Catherine Besteman's *Unraveling Somalia: Race, Violence, and the Legacy of Slavery* (University of Pennsylvania Press, 1999).

### Chapter 5. Foreigner

The stories about Abdulahi in South Africa and during his trip to seek asylum in the United States come from my interviews of him. In South Africa, asylum seekers like Abdulahi did not have a right to marry until a ruling by the South African Supreme Court of Appeals in 2019. The citation for the court decision is *Mzalisi NO & others v. O & another* (630/2018) (2019) ZASCA 138 (October 1, 2019). Judge

Arrington's reference to a 2014 South African Supreme Court of Appeals decision upholding the right of migrants to hold business licenses is to a case discussed in the U.S. Department of State's 2015 Country Report on Human Rights Practices in South Africa. That report also states that the police "illegally targeted" shop owners who, like Abdulahi, were foreigners.

In the South African movement to topple apartheid, protest has played a key role. Although much collective political action in South Africa has been peaceful, demonstrations have sometimes devolved into mob violence against foreigners. This violence is described in a 2014 report for the Southern African Migration Programme and International Migration Research Centre titled *Xenophobic Violence in South Africa: Denialism, Minimalism, Realism*, by Jonathan Crush and Sujata Ramachandran, and in the 2020 Human Rights Watch report *"They Have Robbed Me of My Life": Xenophobic Violence against Non-nationals in South Africa.*

My sources for the deadly perils of the Darién Gap route to the United States are interviews with Abdulahi as well as Kate Linthicum's December 22, 2016, *Los Angeles Times* article, "Migrants from Around the Globe Are Forging a Grueling Path to the U.S. through the Heart of the Rainforest," and the *California Sunday Magazine* Pulitzer Prize–winning article by Nadja Drost, "When Can We Really Rest?," dated April 2, 2020. The statistic that over 100,000 people had transited the Darién Gap in 2021 comes from the International Organization for Migration's October 22, 2021, article, "IOM Appeals for USD 74.7 M to Provide Humanitarian Assistance for Highly Vulnerable Migrants Transiting the Americas."

## Chapter 6. The Struggle

The description of the ICE Special Response Team comes from ICE's website. The story of violence on the ICE Air flight came from numerous interviews with the detained passengers on the flight. Much of the violence is documented in sworn declarations submitted in the class action case *Ibrahim v. Assistant Field Office Director*, Case No. 17-cv-24574-GAYLES, filed in the Southern District of Florida on December 18, 2017. All documents not filed under seal by the parties and issued by the court in the case are available in the public federal court PACER database. Dr. Stephen Symes submitted a declaration in the case stating that the injuries he observed were consistent with the men's stories about what happened on the flight. The OIG investigative report confirmed the passengers' accounts of the violence, stating that "all but one of the [16] detainee interviews included specific allegations of excessive use of force, pertaining to the use of a full body restraint and/or punching, kicking, or slamming of certain detainees by officers that resulted in injuries such as bruising, swelling, aching, and bleeding. The detainees also alleged that the officers used abusive tactics such as pulling, twisting, or stepping on their restraints to gain compliance."

The OIG investigators also interviewed ICE SRT officers who were on the flight. The report states that the Lead SRT Tactical Supervisor "explained that when an officer would ask a detainee to sit down on the airplane, they would say, 'Sir, I need you to sit.'" The supervisor acknowledged that the "use of touch was also utilized by placing a hand on the detainee's shoulder, then on to an elevated use of force if necessary." He stated that "no detainee was slammed down into his/her seat utilizing this method." The same officer, however, described the Somali men as engaged in an "uprising" or "riot" on the plane and admitted that "some officers may have used a tactic whereas [sic] they step on the chain between the detainees' foot shackles in order to gain distance/compliance with them." The concept of "pain compliance," or using pain to gain control of someone, is a recognized term in law enforcement. For a discussion, see Benjamin I. Whipple's 1991 article, "The Fourth Amendment and the Police Use of Pain Compliance Techniques on Nonviolent Arrestees," in the *San Diego Law Review*, vol. 28, no. 61. Despite his admission that his team had used physical force, the Lead SRT Tactical Officer stated that use of force paperwork was not completed. According to the officer, none of his team's actions were "considered to be a takedown that would constitute as [sic] an official use of force" because they did not involve a "hard take-down or strike."

Regarding the use of the WRAP straitjacket on a man, the OIG investigative report states that the Lead SRT Tactical Officer said one of his officers "grabbed [the passenger's] shoulders from behind and took him to the ground, where officers applied a full-body restraint to him." Officers stated that they had just been trained on the use of the WRAP the day before the flight departed. The SRT officers did complete use of force paperwork documenting their use of the WRAP.

The OIG investigative report contains contradictory information regarding the functioning of the toilets on the plane. The investigators state that they reviewed an email stating "that the airplane's lavatories were serviced upon arrival [in Senegal] and did not need a second servicing due to its large waste-holding tanks." Elsewhere in the report, however, an officer acknowledged to investigators that "[a] lavatory overflow problem did arise at the very end of the trip pertaining to the human waste compartment of the airplane becoming completely full, and detainees were asked to limit restroom use when possible."

The OIG investigators state in the report that they were "unable to find any written guidance, policy, or instruction relative to lengthy, unexpected, unavoidable flight delays which may require detainees to remain on board an aircraft for an extended period of time." The Unit Chief of ICE Air Operations in Mesa, Arizona, "believed there to be no ICE policies in place for how to handle these types of predicaments regarding international deportation flights due to the multitude of unpredictable variables that could come into play with each one." The officer "recalled ICE possibly attempting to have a Standard Operating Procedure in place for these flights, but they were discarded due to the impossibility of adhering to them."

## Chapter 7. Glades County Jail

The statistics on the population and income data of Moore Haven, Florida, come from the 2020 U.S. Census. Zora Neale Hurston's description of Lake Okeechobee appears in her 1937 novel, *Their Eyes Were Watching God* (Lippincott). The story of Big Sugar in the region can be found in Amy Green's *Moving Water: The Everglades and Big Sugar* (Johns Hopkins University Press, 2021). Alec Wilkinson's *Big Sugar: Seasons in the Cane Fields of Florida* (Knopf, 1989) describes the sugar industry and the area around Clewiston, Florida. The quote about how cane workers were treated "like slaves" comes from Alec Wilkinson's article, "Big Sugar-II," in the July 24, 1989, *New Yorker*.

Information about the Glades Correctional Development Corporation and the finances of the corporation comes from the Glades County Commission meeting minutes on February 14, 2017, December 12, 2017, and February 26, 2018; the July 5, 2018, article by Jacob Kang-Brown and Jack Norton of the Vera Institute, "More Than a Jail: Immigrant Detention and the Smell of Money"; and Americans for Immigrant Justice and the Southern Poverty Law Center, *Prison by Any Other Name: A Report on South Florida Detention Facilities* (2019). The Internal Revenue Service notice acknowledging that the main purpose of the jail is to detain people for ICE is a letter from Janae R. Lemley of the U.S. Department of Treasury, January 26, 2017, to the Glades Correctional Development Corporation. On February 1, 2022, 17 members of the U.S. House of Representatives wrote a letter to the Department of Homeland Security encouraging them to close Glades County jail. Currently, there are no people being detained by ICE at the jail.

## Chapter 8. Krome Service Processing Center

My sources for the history of the Krome Service Processing Center include Cheryl Little and Joan Friedland, *Krome's Invisible Prisoners: Cycles of Abuse and Neglect*

(Florida Immigrant Advocacy Center, July 1996); Minnesota Lawyers International Human Rights Committee and Physicians for Human Rights, *Hidden from View: Human Rights Conditions in the Krome Detention Center* (April 1991); and Office of the Inspector General, Department of Justice, *Alleged Deception of Congress: The Congressional Task Force on Immigration Reform's Fact-finding Visit to the Miami District of INS in June, 1995* (June 1996). Alfonso Chardy's December 18, 2007, *Miami Herald* article, "Krome Gets a Makeover," describes Krome's "new medical clinic" and quotes the Florida Field Office Director for ICE as saying, "The average person that lives in the state of Florida doesn't receive this level [of medical care] on the initial stages."

The anecdotes about Judge Foster come from my personal observation from appearing before him in court as well as discussions with other lawyers. The statistics about asylum case denial rates, including those of Judge Foster, come from TRAC Immigration, *Asylum Denial Rates by Immigration Judge*, FY 2000–FY 2005. The 1989 legislative report that includes a letter about the judge ordering deported eight people from Haiti in ten minutes without telling them about their right to seek asylum is *Hearing Before the Subcommittee on Immigration, Refugees, and International Law of the Committee on the Judiciary*, House of Representatives, 101st Congress, 1st Session, June 8, 1989, vol. 4. The 1995 Public Health Service Clinic chief's statement about Krome and the admonishment from the government accountability office are referenced in Cheryl Little's *Written Testimony Before the Subcommittee on Immigration, Citizenship, Refugees, Border Security, and International Law of the Committee on the Judiciary, House of Representatives, "Detention and Removal: Immigration Detainee Medical Care,"* 110th Congress, 1st Session, October 4, 2007, vol. 4, page 93. For more on the pre-2005 years of immigration detention, including Krome, see *American Gulag: Inside U.S. Immigration Prisons* (University of California Press, 2004), by Mark Dow.

Rahim Mohamed made his public statements about the ICE Air flight to Carlos Ballesteros at *Newsweek,* which published them in the article "ICE Kept 92 Immigrants Shackled on a Plane for Two Days in 'Slave Ship' Conditions, Advocates Say," December 14, 2017. ICE's official blanket denial came from Public Affairs Officer/Spokesperson Brendan Raedy in a December 13, 2017, email to Carlos Ballesteros and states:

> Upon landing for a refueling and pilot exchange at Dakar, Senegal, ICE was notified that the relief crew was unable to get sufficient crew rest due to issues with their hotel in Dakar. The aircraft, including the detainees and crew on board, remained parked at the airport to allow the relief crew time to rest.

During this time, the aircraft maintained power and air conditioning, and was stocked with sufficient food and water. Detainees were fed at regular intervals to include the providing of extra snacks and drinks. Lavatories were functional and serviced the entire duration of the trip. The allegations of ICE mistreatment onboard the Somali flight are categorically false. No one was injured during the flight, and there were no incidents or altercations that would have caused any injuries on the flight.

ICE's official statement contradicts the statements of the Somali passengers and the OIG investigative report's later documentation of an "uprising" or "riot." The OIG report contains no explanation of this inconsistency.

## Chapter 9. Stay of Deportation

The definition of "stay" comes from *Black's Law Dictionary*, 11th ed. (Thomson Reuters, 2019). A compilation of letters documenting the abusive language and poor conditions at Glades is available on the website of the Immigration Clinic of the University of Miami School of Law. Similar findings appear in the December 9, 2019, report by Americans for Immigrant Justice and the Southern Poverty Law Center, *Prison by Any Other Name: A Report on South Florida Detention Facilities*. A summary of complaints filed against Glades appears in the January 24, 2022, letter of the American Civil Liberties Union Foundation of Florida to the Acting Director of U.S. Immigration and Customs Enforcement.

News articles about U.S. District Court Judge Darrin P. Gayles include the June 17, 2014, *Miami Herald* article "Miami's Gayles Confirmed as First Openly Gay Black Male Judge." The case number for the class action lawsuit *Ibrahim v. Assistant Field Office Director* is Case No. 17-cv-24574-GAYLES, filed in the Southern District of Florida on December 18, 2017. All documents not under seal filed by the parties and issued by the court in the case are available in the federal court PACER database.

Court-filed declarations from passengers on the ICE Air flight discuss the use of the WRAP straitjacket, nicknamed "burrito." The use of the WRAP straitjacket was confirmed in interviews of men who were sitting in the back of the plane and by officers interviewed during the OIG investigation. The investigative report states that a man, presumably Farrah Ibrahim, the lead plaintiff in the class action lawsuit, was put in the WRAP restraint for over two hours. On October 13, 2021, a coalition of groups filed a complaint with the Office for Civil Rights and Civil Liberties of the U.S. Department of Homeland Security on behalf of individuals who have been subjected to the full-body restraint in a variety of contexts.

The statement that Somalia was having "one of the worst humanitarian crises in the world" comes from the U.S. government's January 17, 2017, *Federal Register* notice renewing Temporary Protected Status to certain Somalis in the United States based on the severe level of danger. The citation to the U.S. district court decision in *Brown v. Board of Education* referencing the plaintiffs' request for a permanent injunction restraining enforcement of the state statute allowing for segregation of educational facilities is *Brown v. Board of Education of Topeka*, 98 F. Supp. 797 (D. Kan. 1951). In *Bush v. Gore*, 531 U.S. 98 (2000), the U.S. Supreme Court granted the campaign of President Bush a stay of the Florida Supreme Court's recount of ballots in Florida.

Judge Gayles's statements during the January 8, 2018, hearing come from the official court transcript, available on the federal court PACER database.

## Chapter 10. Jurisdiction

The definition of subject matter jurisdiction comes from the legal treatise *Federal Practice and Procedure* (Thomson Reuters, 1986–2023), by Charles A. Wright and Arthur R. Miller. This treatise is also the source of the quote about the importance of subject matter jurisdiction. For more on the background of the U.S. Supreme Court case *Marbury v. Madison*, see William E. Nelson, *Marbury v. Madison: The Origins and Legacy of Judicial Review* (University Press of Kansas, 2000).

The quotes from the January 8, 2018, hearing before Judge Gayles on jurisdiction come from the official court transcript, available on the federal court database PACER. Also on PACER are Judge Gayles's January 26, 2018, order finding he had subject matter jurisdiction and his June 21, 2018, order certifying the lawsuit as a class action.

The email regarding Abdulahi being on crutches and needing an MRI is on file with the author.

## Chapter 11. Contempt of Court

The definition of "contempt power" is from *Black's Law Dictionary*, 11th ed. (Thomson Reuters, 2019). The Christmas morning pepper spray incident is discussed at length in the legal team's January 8, 2018, administrative complaint filed with the Office of Inspector General of the Department of Homeland Security and the Office of Civil Rights and Civil Liberties of the U.S. Department of Homeland Security, available on the website of the Immigration Clinic of the University of Miami School of Law. The quotes describing the effects of pepper spray come from the U.S. Court of Appeals for the Ninth Circuit's 2000 opinion in *Headwaters Forest Def. v. County of Humboldt*. Pepper spray qualifies as a riot-control agent as defined by the 1993 Chemical Weapons Convention. The Convention bans the use of riot-control agents as a method of warfare.

In 2015, Congress passed the Eric Williams Correctional Officer Protection Act to authorize the Director of the Bureau of Prisons to use pepper spray. Even before the legislation, Department of Justice officers were authorized to use pepper spray. The February 3, 1999, decision in the border patrol union case protesting the requirement that an officer be pepper sprayed as a precondition to using it on others is available on the website of the U.S. Federal Labor Relations Authority. The story of a detained person dying after being pepper sprayed is reported in Julie K. Brown's article, "As Florida Inmate Begged for Help, Guards Gassed Him to Death, Suit Says," in the *Miami Herald* on September 20, 2016. For letters objecting to the historical misuse of pepper spray at Glades, see the website of the Immigration Clinic of the University of Miami School of Law. A copy of the memorandum of the officer in charge of Glades to the Immigration Clinic of the University of Miami School of Law is on the same web page. The name of the officer in charge has been changed, like the names of many others in this book.

On January 4, 2018, Dr. Stephen Symes of the University of Miami School of Medicine wrote a sworn declaration describing the injuries of 18 individuals he examined. This sworn declaration was attached to the administrative complaint against Glades, available on the website of the Immigration Clinic of the University of Miami School of Law. Dr. Symes's January 29, 2018, sworn declaration detailing his assessment of Sa'id's injured hand spells Sa'id's last name as "Jamale" instead of "Janale." The quote from the declaration corrects this misspelling. The declaration was filed under seal in *Ibrahim v. Assistant Field Office Director*, Case No. 17-cv-24574-GAYLES, filed in the Southern District of Florida on December 18, 2017.

The 2008 *Washington Post* investigative series about poor medical care in immigration detention is "Careless Detention." The quote about 1.3 million dollars being saved by denying medical care comes from U.S. Representative Zoe Lofgren's statement summarizing the findings of the *Washington Post*. She made her statements at the June 4, 2008, Hearing Before the Subcommittee on Immigration, Citizenship, Refugees, Border Security, and International Law of the Committee on the Judiciary, House of Representatives. Human Rights Watch authored a 2009 report on health care in immigration detention: *U.S.: Immigration Detention Neglects Health*. The Florida Immigrant Advocacy Center's February 2009 report, *Dying for Decent Care: Bad Medicine in Immigration Custody*, discusses the denial of medical care in detention centers, including in Florida.

A source of information about deaths of people in ICE custody is the article "Mapping Factors Associated with Deaths in Immigration Detention in the United States, 2011–2018: A Thematic Analysis," by Parveen Parmar, Madeline Ross, Sophie Terp, Naomi Kearl, Briah Fischer, Molly Grassini, Sameer Ahmed, Niels Frenzen, and Elizabeth Burner, in *Lancet Regional Health—Americas* 2 (October 2021). Since 2018, ICE has been reporting the deaths of people in its custody on its website. Deaths since 2015 can be found on the website of the American Immigration Lawyers Association. For reporting of deaths between 2003 and 2013, see ICE's Freedom of Information Act response, *List of Deaths in ICE Custody: October 2003–December 2, 2013*, on ICE's website.

The quoted law treatise on the concept of contempt of court is *The American Law Register*, published in 1881. My source on the historical use of contempt power is John Charles Fox's 1908 article "King v. Almon II" in *Law Quarterly Review*. The relevant Federal Rule of Civil Procedure on contempt of court is Rule 70, titled "Enforcing a Judgment for a Specific Act." The rule permits a judge to hold a "disobedient party" in contempt. The July 9, 2018, email to the legal team characterizing the sit-down with the government over medical issues as a "sham" is on file with the author.

The incidents involving Agane and other Somali men in the SHU in February 2018 are documented in court filings in the class action lawsuit filed on February 11, 2018, and in interviews with Sa'id. The names of the officers have been changed. The email documenting the verbal warning to ICE's attorneys that "someone might die," the email about how the abuse at Glades had reached a "breaking point," the email from the wife of a detained man about the abuse in the SHU, and an email documenting Janene's call on the same topic are on file with the author. The quotes from the February 14, 2018, hearing before Judge Gayles on the motion for contempt are from the official court transcript.

## Chapter 12. Motion to Reopen

The definition of "reopen" is from *Black's Law Dictionary*, 11th ed. (Thomson Reuters, 2019). The description of a motion to reopen as a "safety valve" comes from the Ninth Circuit case *Salim v. Lynch*, 831 F.3d 1133, 1137 (9th Cir. 2016). The regulation governing reopening is chapter 8 of the Code of Federal Regulations section 1003.2(c)(3)(ii). The letters from the four detained men who wanted to be released from the lawsuit and deported are on the federal court database PACER. The request for five contact rooms for legal meetings at Glades and the discussion of the inability of the legal team to prepare the motions to reopen without the immigration files of the Somali men and women comes from the legal team's motion for contempt filed on January 17, 2018, available on PACER. Judge Gayles's February 1, 2018, order requiring the government to turn over the files of the people on the flight within 15 days and his March 9, 2018, order to provide reasonable access to attorneys, including contact rooms, are on PACER. The difficulties faced by the lawyers in getting access to their clients at Glades is described in numerous affidavits filed with Judge Gayles, also available on PACER. The quotes from the legal team and Judge Gayles in court are from the court's official transcript for the November 20, 2018, hearing. The statement that no nurse wanted to meet with Abdulahi because he had too many issues is documented in a filing submitted by the legal team to the court on November 14, 2018.

## Chapter 13. Day In Court

All dialogue during Sa'id's immigration hearing from the moment that the judge entered the courtroom are quotes from the official court recording of the hearing. The recording is on file with the author. Additional information about what happened the day of Sa'id's court hearing came from Sa'id, his wife Janene, and his lawyer, Andrea Montavon-McKillip.

## Chapter 14. Journey's End

Information about conditions at Stewart Detention Center came from the 2012 report *Expose and Close,* published by the Detention Watch Network, as well as the 2019 article "A Snapshot of Immigration Court at Stewart Detention Center," by Lauren Ricciardelli, Larry Nackerud, Katherine Cochrane, India Sims, Latifa Crawford, and Demetria Taylor, published in *Critical Social Work,* vol. 20, no. 1. On October 11, 2019, a group of people detained at Stewart filed a complaint with the Department of Homeland Security's Office for Civil Rights and Civil Liberties reporting abuses at the detention center. This complaint is available on the website of the Detention Watch Network.

The information regarding the statistics of the judges at Stewart come from the Transactional Records Access Clearinghouse and the December 12, 2016, article by Christie Thompson of the Marshall Project, "America's Toughest Immigration Court: Welcome to Stewart Detention Center, the Black Hole of the Immigration System." The August 8, 2017, letter from the Southern Poverty Law Center was addressed to the Acting Director of the Executive Office for Immigration Review, which is part of the U.S. Department of Justice. All quotes from the moment the two immigration judges went on the record in the hearings on Abdulahi's asylum case are from the official court transcript. The quotes from Judge Arrington's denial of Abdulahi's asylum case come from the decision itself. The information about Judge Trimble's background comes from his official biography with the Executive Office of Immigration Review and the Fiscal Year Reports of the Board of Visitors for the Western Hemisphere Institute for Security Cooperation. The quote from the expert on country conditions comes from the declaration of Stig Jarle Hansen of the Institute of International, Environment, and Development Studies at the Norwegian University of Life Sciences.

## Epilogue

The "deporter-in-chief" moniker for President Obama appeared widely in the press, including in NBC's April 17, 2015, article by Amanda Sakuma, "Obama Leaves Behind a Mixed Legacy on Immigration." The detention statistics come from ICE's website and the website of the Transactional Records Access Clearinghouse, housed at Syracuse University.

ICE's lie about the reason for the plane being stuck on the tarmac in Senegal and the quotes from officers (and at least one nurse) on the ICE Air flight come from the OIG's investigative report into the flight. The quote about the Assistant Attaché not requesting permission for the plane passengers to disembark is also from the report.

The quote from Frederick Douglass comes from his 1845 book *Narrative of the Life of Frederick Douglass: An American Slave*. The October 19, 2021, *New York Times* article, "Images of Border Patrol's Treatment of Haitian Migrants Prompt Outrage," discusses how border agents on horseback used lassos on people from Haiti and includes photographs documenting the practice.

# Index

*Note: Maps and figures are denoted with f after the page number.*

arguments over jail telephone, 118–19. *See also* Christmas Day incident

arrests, 3, 19, 71, 134, 188

Arrington, Judge Saundra D., 161–62, 163, 164, 165, 167, 173

art, 4–5

Article 33 of Convention Relating to the Status of Refugees, 11–12

Asha, 33, 40

Assistant U.S. Attorney, 105, 128. *See also* U.S. Attorney's Office

asylum: application for, 10–11, 12, 64–65, 81, 92; cases, 12, 76, 109, 112, 136–38, 144, 159, 160, 161; firm resettlement as barrier to, 157, 163–64, 165, 166; grounds for, 12; hearings of Abdulahi, 161–63, 168, 169, 170–74; seekers, 68–70, 72, 89, 90, 101; system, 12, 176

attorney access, 107, 112, 133–34, 139–40, 207

Authorized Restraint Devices, 13

baby, death of, 44

Bajuni people, 33, 40

Ballesteros, Carlos, 91

bariis ishkukaris, 64

Barre, Siad, 37, 38, 52–53, 57

bathrooms: in detention centers, 8, 86, 100, 158; on Flight N225AX, 27–28, 30, 91, 103; in solitary confinement, 121, 130, 131

BBC, 104, 180

Beledwyne, Somalia, 49–50, 51, 54, 59

Biden Administration, 183

birthdates, 57

Black students, 47

Blaise Diagne International Airport, 22

Board of Immigration Appeals, 138, 142, 143, 144, 175. *See also* appeals

boat travel, 4–5, 33, 35–36, 40–41, 72–74

Boston, 19, 156

Boston Immigration Court, 145

Brazil, 71, 72

bribery, 65, 90, 164–65, 171

Britain, 36

British Somaliland, 36

bullying, 18, 47–48, 59

Burundi, 43

Bush Administration, 183

Camp Hagadera, 41

Camp Ifo, 42

Camp Kakuma, 42–45

canjeero, 56

capsaicin, 119

carjacker, 70

case reopenings: of Abdulahi, 136, 138, 144, 160; abuse preventing, 133; definition, 135; difficulty of, 103–4, 141; as goal of class action lawsuit, 182–83; process of, 136, 138–39; right to seek, 101; of Sa'id, 145–46; from Somalia, 111–12, 115–16; success rates of, 140–41; volunteer lawyers to help with, 114

Casper, Ben, 180, 181

caste, 54

cattle grazing, 44

celebration meal, 154–56

cellphones, 72, 74, 90, 187

cerebral palsy, 6

changed circumstances, 112–13, 136, 166

Chemical Weapons Convention, 119

Christmas Day incident, 117–18, 134

civil immigration system, 119

civil war in Somalia, 31–48; arriving in Kismayo, 35–36; causes of, 36–38

clan affiliation: civil war and, 36–38; danger posed by, 164–65, 173;

description of, 49, 54; family of
  Abdulahi, 59
clan militias: Abdulahi in danger
  from, 173, 176; impact on Abdulahi's family, 56–57, 60–61, 152;
  starting civil war, 31, 38–40
class action certification, 116, 181
class action lawsuits, 116, 142–43,
  180–82. *See also Ibrahim v. Assistant*
  *Field Office Director*
Classic Air Charter, 16
cleaning in detention centers, 13, 100,
  131. *See also* detention centers
Clewiston, Florida, 83
coal mining, 63–64
Cold War, 37, 38
colonialism, legacy of in Somalia, 37
colonization, 36–37
conditions of refugee camps, 43
Congo, refugees from, 43
construction jobs, 19
contact rooms, 140, 147
contempt power, 117, 127, 133
Convention Relating to the Status of
  Refugees. *See* United Nations
  Convention Relating to the Status
  of Refugees
CoreCivic, 157
coronavirus, 175
corporal punishment, 18, 47
correctional officers, 90, 92, 118–19
Corrections Corporation of America,
  76, 157, 158
court decisions, 115–16, 146, 154, 159,
  162–65, 174–75
court hearings: attempts to secure, 103,
  123, 136; final for Abdulahi, 167–74;
  final for Sa'id, 146–48; held by Judge
  Arrington, 161–62, 165; held by
  Judge Gayles, 105, 108, 111–13, 133,
  143; held by Judge Lopez-Enriquez,

151–54; held by Judge Trimble,
  167–74; Sa'id denied, 20
courtrooms, 108–9, 147–49, 169–70
criminal status, 18–20, 100, 150–51, 153
cross-examination, 147, 153, 174
crowdfunding campaign, 186–87
Crumine, Andrea, 181
CSI Aviation, 16
Cuban missile crisis, 89
cultural adjustment, 18

Dadaab refugee camp, 41
Dakar, Senegal, 22, 29, 77
Dallas, Texas, 45, 47, 152
Darién Gap, 72, 74–75
Darod clan, 54
Day, Judge Steven, 20, 145
deaths in detention, 126, 129
deaths in Somalia, 4, 39, 40, 61, 152
debt, 25, 64
deception, 21, 32, 77, 91, 184
declarations, written, 150, 180
De Leon, Alexandra, 181
delivery driving, 69–70
Department of Homeland Security,
  129, 132, 134
deportation: anticipation of, 6–7; on
  Flight N225AX, 4; hours leading up
  to, 14–16; lawyers working to stop,
  95, 101; order for, 20, 21, 163, 174;
  second flight halted, 107, 111, 116;
  without travel documents, 9, 21. *See*
  *also* Flight N225AX
detention: of Abdulahi upon arrival in
  U.S., 76; Abdulahi waiting in, 169,
  175–76; at Glades County Detention Center, 82–87; at Krome
  Service Processing Center, 88–95;
  medical care in, 124–28; political
  aspects of, 183; prior to Flight
  N225AX, 3–4, 8, 10, 12–13; safety

detention *(continued)*
  and abuse in, 128–34; solitary
  confinement in, 117–23, 129–34; at
  Stewart Detention Center, 157–59
detention centers: abuse and
  conditions in, 86, 90, 100, 118–34,
  137, 158–59; deaths in, 126;
  expansion of, 183; for immigrants,
  7–8; schedules of, 99. *See also*
  Alexandria Staging Facility; Glades
  County Detention Center; Krome
  Service Processing Center; Stewart
  Detention Center
Detention Watch Network, 158
Digil clan, 54
Dir clan, 54
direct examination, 151, 172
discretionary waiver, 151
discrimination, 54. *See also* racism
Djibouti, 24
DooDoo bug, 43
Douglass, Frederick, 185
drugs, 90
dugsi, an Islamic school, 31–32, 38–39
Duvalier, Jean-Claude "Baby Doc,"
  89. *See also* Haiti; Haitian asylum
  seekers

education, 56–58. *See also* schools
emergency stays of removal, 143
Emory University School of
  Medicine, 15
English language, 57
entrepreneurs, 65
Eritrea, 74
Ethiopia, 35f, 36, 37, 43, 57

family ties, 151
Fardowso: Abdulahi's decision to leave
  South Africa with, 70–71; Abdulahi's
  photo of, 160; Abdulahi updated

about, 188; decision to stay in South
  Africa of, 72; funds from, 75; initial
  meeting and pregnancy, 68–69; loss
  of contact with, 28, 136, 176
fear of returning home, 11, 65, 136,
  166, 173
Federal Bureau of Investigation (FBI),
  90
*Federal Practice and Procedure* (Wright
  and Miller), 108
fetters, 13
Fifth Amendment, U.S. Constitution,
  112, 115
firm resettlement, 157, 164, 165
fishermen, 5, 33, 35–36
fleeing Somalia, 40–41, 62, 63–64
flight brokers, 16
flight delays. *See* Flight N225AX
Flight N225AX: abuse allegations of,
  102–3, 105; demands of passengers
  on, 26, 77; deportation orders of
  others on, 150; experience of,
  77–81, 91, 101, 102–3; grounded in
  Dakar, 22–24, 25–30, 77–81; initial
  take off of, 4; injuries from, 78, 80,
  102–3, 126, 127; media coverage of,
  104; reasons for grounding, 23, 26,
  184; to return to the United States,
  80–82, 88; route of, 85f; second
  flight stopped by lawsuit, 182–83;
  sworn declarations about events
  of, 95
flight nurses, 24, 26, 79, 184.
Florida Immigrant Advocacy Center,
  90. *See also* Americans for
  Immigrant Justice
food, 27, 41, 42, 56, 100, 106, 158
Fort Benning, Georgia, 165
Foster, Judge Neale Strong, 89
Freedom of Information Act, 139, 203
Fuad, 130

Garad, Hassan Mohumed, 54–55, 57–58, 60, 64

Gayles, Judge Darrin P.: background of, 102; contempt powers of, 127, 133; dismissing class action lawsuit, 142; enforcing treatment of injuries, 127; hearing *Ibrahim v. Assistant Field Officer Director*, 103–7, 108, 112–13; order for detainees to have legal visits, 140; ruling of, 115–16; subject matter jurisdiction and, 111

genealogy, 54

genocide, 11

GEO Group, 8, 83

Glades Correctional Development Corporation (GCDC), 84

Glades County, Florida, 83–84

Glades County Detention Center: abuse at, 130–33; administrative complaint filed against, 129; arrival at, 85–86; background on, 83; Kevin Harris in charge of, 122–23, 140; legal visits at, 140; Sa'id at, 128–29, 145; Sa'id released from, 156; schedule of, 99; use of pepper spray in, 118–20, 121; women moved to, 90

Gonzalez, Ms., 121

government delays, 139, 140

hair, 55

Haiti, 89

Haitian asylum seekers, 89, 186

Hamdi, 51–52, 56, 60–62, 94, 188

handcuffs, 13–14, 15, 121, 195. *See also* shackles

hand injury, Sa'id's, 4, 78, 80, 118, 124, 124f, 126–27, 128

hard hair, 55

Harper, Mary, 180

Harris, Kevin, 122–23, 140

Hartmann, Lily, 181

Hassan, Abdirahman Abdulahi, 72

Hawadle clan, 54, 55, 56, 59, 63, 165, 166

Hawiye clan, 38, 49, 54, 55, 165, 167

Hernandez, Tatiana, 181

Hiatt company, 13–14

Hiatt-Thompson 2010 Chain Link Cuffs, 13

hijacking of fishing boat, 38

homes, 50–51

hope, 29, 95

hospitality, Kantian principle of, 11

houses, 43, 50–51, 60–62, 63

human rights principles, 10–11

hunger, 41, 43, 75, 100

Hurston, Zora Neale, 83

hydration, 27

Ibrahim, 24, 79, 88, 92, 95, 138, 160

Ibrahim, Farah, 89, 101, 102

*Ibrahim v. Assistant Field Office Director*: assigned to Judge Gayles, 102; court order in, 115–16; hearing of, 103–7, 108–9, 111; purpose of, 101

ICE Air flights, 7, 14–15, 182–84. *See also* Flight N225AX

ICE Assistant Attaché for Removals, 185

Ifraah, 65, 67–68, 69, 113

illness, 75

immigrant detention centers. *See* detention centers

Immigration and Customs Enforcement (ICE): attorney for, 102, 105, 111, 128, 134, 139–40, 148, 150, 153, 172, 181; building Stewart Detention Center, 158; bus arrival, 86; carrying out deportations, 143;

45; relief of, 107; resources upon arriving in Somalia, 23–24; school attack of, 38–39; sketch of, 34f; in solitary confinement, 122–23, 128–29; struggle of on deportation flight, 79–80; tattoo of, 125f
Janene: contacting lawyers, 101; experiences of, 153; having two children with Sa'id, 186; introduction to, 6–7; photo with Sa'id, 155f; positive influence of, 23; Sa'id calling on the phone, 117, 132; Sa'id meeting, 19; seeing at court hearing, 149; sharing good news with, 145–46; worry of, 20–21
jareer, 55
Jefferson, Thomas, 110
jileec, 55
jobs, 56–58, 60
Johannesburg, 65
Johnson, Lyndon B., 11
Jubba Airways, 24
Jubba River, 49
judicial authority, 109–10
jungle travel, 74–75
juries, 149
jurisdiction, 109–11, 112, 115. *See also* subject matter jurisdiction

Kant, Immanuel, 11
Kenya, 35f, 187
Khadija, 19, 146
Kibajuni language, 33
Kismayo, Somalia, 31, 33, 35, 38
knee injury, Abdulahi's, 113–14, 116, 135, 137, 141–42, 167, 188
Krome Service Processing Center: Abdulahi detained at, 88; Ibrahim's release from, 160; immigration court at, 146, 150; legal visits at, 92, 116; in Miami, 82, 89; nurses at, 142;

reputation of, 89–90; request for transfer to, 133, 134
Kwerekwere (derogatory term), 63, 66

Lake Okeechobee, 83
lashes, 31, 33. *See also* whips
lawsuits: calling for medical treatment, 133–34; closed, 143; filed as *Ibrahim v. Assistant Field Office Director*, 102–3; news spreading of, 95, 101, 106; opting out of, 114–15, 138. See also *Ibrahim v. Assistant Field Office Director*
lawyer, Abdulahi's, 161–62, 167–68, 170, 171, 173, 174, 175
lawyer, Sa'id's, 147, 149, 152
lawyers mobilizing to help, 90–95, 101, 114, 123–27, 179, 180–81
Layla, 18
League of Nations Convention Relating to the International Status of Refugees, 11
Legal Aid Service of Broward County, 181
legal arguments, 103–6, 109, 111–12, 115–16, 118–19, 143, 163–67, 171–75
legal files, 139, 146–47
legal histories, 139
legal visits: with Abdulahi, 93–94, 114, 137–38, 141, 176; difficulty of, 139; with Ibrahim, 95; with medical professionals, 123; with Sa'id, 147. *See also* attorney access
Lehner, Lisa, 181
Lerner, Romy, 179
lies, 77, 91, 184
litigation, emergency, 182
"Little Mogadishu," 65
loo-maa-oyayaasha (term), 36
looters, 67, 68

deportation, 142; marriage to Fardowso, 69; sense of dehumanization of, 15–16; separated from lawyer and community, 161; sketch of, 53f; at Stewart Detention Center, 158–59; as Sufi Muslim, 51, 166, 167, 171, 173, 174; trauma of, 92, 141, 176; travel to United States, 72–76

Montavon-McKillip, Andrea, 181

Moore Haven, Florida, 83–84

mosquitos, 43

motions to reopen. *See* reopening of cases.

M.S. *St. Louis*, 11

Mubarak, Abdi Janale, 33, 40

Muhammad, son of Abdulahi, 66, 67, 68

Nadim, 23, 78, 81

names, Somali, 54

neglect, 124, 126

news coverage, 91, 95, 104, 113, 126

*Newsweek*, 91, 95

*New York Times*, 104

nightmares, 152

nomads. *See* pastoralists

non-refoulement, 10–11

non-return. *See* non-refoulement

Noor, 45

Nyla, 18

Obama, Barack, 102, 183

ocean, 35–36

Office of Immigration Judges, 161

Office of the Inspector General, 129, 132, 134, 184, 185

officer safety, perceived threats to, 8, 17, 119

Ogaden region, 36, 37, 57

Ogaden War, 37, 38, 57–58

Omar, 9, 26

Omni Air International, 4, 16

oppression under apartheid, 69. *See also* apartheid

Osberg, Carson, 181

Osman, Farah, 62

overcrowding, 90, 128–29

pain: from hand injury of Sa'id, 78, 118, 127; from leg injury of Abdulahi, 67, 92, 113, 136–37, 142, 167; from pepper spray, 119, 120; from shackles, 23, 25, 92, 118, 126

Palladino, Officer, 131

Panama, 75

panga knives, 66

pastoralists, 36, 44

pepper spray, 118–21, 122, 129, 130, 134

permanent residency, 150–51

personal possessions, 159

phone calls, 3–4, 117–18, 128, 132, 136–37, 147

pinky finger injury. *See* hand injury

plaintiffs, 102–3

police, Senegalese, 28, 29, 30

population of refugee camps, 42, 43

pregnancy, 18, 21, 55, 69

prison companies, 8, 83, 157

probation, 19

pro bono lawyers, 114, 138, 143

protection law, 10–11

Protocol Relating to the Status of Refugees, 11–12

Public Health Service Clinic, 90

Qanyare, Ali, 60–61

quiet, lack of in detention centers, 12, 100, 116

Qur'an, 13, 31–32, 39

racism, 16, 17, 99, 129, 130, 184, 185–86. *See also* apartheid

Somali Embassy, 9, 20, 77, 93
Somali immigrants as entrepreneurs, 65
Somali language, 5–6, 33
"Somali 9/11," 5
Somali Republic, 37
South Africa: Abdulahi's arrival in, 63; Abdulahi's wive's in, 64–72, 94; asylum seekers not safe in, 70; experiences in, 173; perceived safety in, 176; temporary refugee status in, 163–64, 165, 166, 171, 174
Southern Poverty Law Center, 161
South Sudanese children, 43
Soviet Union, 37
Special Housing Unit (SHU), 117, 121–22, 128–29, 130, 132. *See also* solitary confinement
Special Response Team (SRT), 16–17, 78, 79, 80, 82
stay of deportation, 99, 105–7, 109, 111–16, 140, 143
stereotypes, 184
Stewart Detention Center: Abdulahi at, 116, 144, 157, 176; background on, 76; coronavirus at, 175; descriptions of, 159–60; Jane McPherson volunteering at, 186; opening of, 158
stories, telling, 170–71
straitjackets, 17, 80, 101, 102
strip searches, 147
subclans, 52–54
subject matter jurisdiction, 106, 108, 109. *See also* jurisdiction
Sudan, 43
Suffolk County jail, 20, 124
Sufi Muslims, 51, 166, 171, 174
sugar cane, cutting, 83–84
sugar industry, 83

Supreme Court of Appeal of South Africa, 164
surbiyaan hilib adhi, 56
Swahili language, 33
SWAT team, 16–17
swimming, 4, 49, 50, 52, 72–74, 163
swing cuffs, 14. *See also* handcuffs
sworn declarations, 95
Symes, Dr. Stephen, 25, 123, 124, 126–27, 128

tattoos, 5, 125f, 152
telephones. *See* phone calls
tents, 5, 41–42
terrorism, 38, 104
testimonies, 12, 103, 151, 154, 162, 165, 168–69, 172–74
Texas, 5, 18, 19, 47, 125f, 149, 152
Tiffany, 18, 146
timelines for filing motions to reopen, 114–15
"Tippy Toes," 120
toilets. *See* bathrooms
Toyi Toyi chants, 67
traffic tickets, 84
transport hoods, 16–17
trauma, 61, 92, 113, 150, 152, 168
travel documents, 9, 20, 21
Trimble, Judge Dan, 165–66, 167–68, 169–71, 172, 173
Truman, President, 11
Trump Administration, 8, 85, 183, 186
Turkana people, 44

Uganda, refugees from, 43
United Nations, 11, 29, 77, 184
United Nations Convention Relating to the Status of Refugees, 11, 41
United Nations High Commissioner for Refugees, 42–43, 45